Lecture Notes in Computer Science   13297

More information about this series at https://link.springer.com/bookseries/558

Gilles Perrouin · Naouel Moha ·
Abdelhak-Djamel Seriai (Eds.)

Reuse and Software Quality

20th International Conference
on Software and Systems Reuse, ICSR 2022
Montpellier, France, June 15–17, 2022
Proceedings

Editors
Gilles Perrouin 🆔
University of Namur
Namur, Belgium

Naouel Moha 🆔
École de Technologie Supérieure
Montreal, QC, Canada

Abdelhak-Djamel Seriai 🆔
University of Montpellier
Montpellier, France

ISSN 0302-9743   ISSN 1611-3349 (electronic)
Lecture Notes in Computer Science
ISBN 978-3-031-08128-6   ISBN 978-3-031-08129-3 (eBook)
https://doi.org/10.1007/978-3-031-08129-3

This Springer imprint is published by the registered company Springer Nature Switzerland AG
The registered company address is: Gewerbestrasse 11, 6330 Cham, Switzerland

Preface

This volume contains the proceedings of the 20th edition of the International Conference on Software and Systems Reuse (ICSR 2022). This volume was prepared jointly by the program chairs (Gilles Perrouin, Naouel Moha) and the general chair (Abdelhak-Djamel Seriai). The conference was initially planned to be held in Montpellier, France, during June 15–17, 2022. Though the world was hoping to see the end of this COVID-19 pandemic many uncertainties remained that could prevent attendees from travelling to the conference. The organization team therefore opted for a virtual format once again. This format has the advantage of making the conference accessible to everyone.

ICSR is the premier international event in the software reuse community. The main goal of ICSR is to present the most recent advances in the area of software and systems reuse and to promote an exchange of ideas and best practices among researchers and practitioners.

The chosen theme for this anniversary edition was "reuse and software quality". Indeed, the reuse of robust, validated components and libraries is a blessing for the software community who can quickly build high-quality applications. But this is also a curse if one of the links in the software supply chain is not up to standard, endangering the whole ecosystem depending on it. We also welcomed papers on every aspect of software reuse, be it technical or managerial (e.g., handling open-source licenses).

We adopted a two-phase submission process requiring abstracts one week prior to the full paper submission deadline. Following the current practices in reviewing, we also kept the double-blind process. We received 28 full and one short complete submissions, out of which six were accepted as full papers, one was accepted as full paper after shepherding, and two were retained for publication as short papers. The full paper acceptance rate was 25% (7/28) and the overall acceptance rate was 31% (9/29).

This anniversary edition both looked at the past and to the future of the conference. We were delighted to have Bill Frakes, one of the founding members of the conference, who delivered the following keynote: "Software Reuse and Domain Engineering – Industry Impact and Future". The second keynote speaker, Ying (Jenny) Zou, offered us a keynote entitled "Intelligent Management of Code Clones". This edition also featured panels on the future, security, and sustainable software reuse.

We would like to thank the ICSR steering committee (notably Rafael Capilla and Hafedh Mili) and the local organization team for the virtualization of the conference.

May 2022

Gilles Perrouin
Naouel Moha
Abdelhak-Djamel Seriai

Organization

General Chair

Abdelhak-Djamel Seriai   University of Montpellier, France

Program Committee Chairs

Gilles Perrouin   University of Namur, Belgium
Naouel Moha   Ecole de technologie supérieure - Université du
     Québec, Canada

Workshop and Tutorial Co-chairs

Christophe Dony   University of Montpellier, France
Mohamed Wiem Mkaouer   Rochester Institute of Technology, USA

Doctoral Symposium Co-chairs

Bedir Tekinerdogan   Wageningen University, The Netherlands
Christelle Urtado   EuroMov-DHM, University of Montpellier and
     IMT Mines Alès, France

Industry Panel Chair

Tewfik Ziadi   Sorbonne University, France

Demonstration and Tools Chair

Chouki Tibermacine   University of Montpellier, France

Publicity Chair

Marianne Huchard   University of Montpellier, France

Local Organization Co-chairs

Hinde Bouziane   University of Montpellier, France
Sylvain Vauttier   EuroMov DHM, University of Montpellier and
     IMT Mines Alès, France

Web and Media Co-chairs

David Delahaye   University of Montpellier, France
Sylvain Vauttier   EuroMov DHM, University of Montpellier and
                                  IMT Mines Alès, France

Green Conference Co-chairs

Clémentine Nebut   University of Montpellier, France
Marianne Huchard   University of Montpellier, France

Steering Committee

Rafael Capilla Sevilla   Universidad Rey Juan Carlos, Spain
Hafedh Mili   Université du Québec à Montréal, Canada
Claudia M. L. Werner   Federal University of Rio de Janeiro, Brazil
Martin L. Griss   Carnegie Mellon University, USA
William B. Frakes   IEEE TCSE Committee on Software Reuse, USA
John Favaro   Trust-IT, Italy
Eduardo Almeida   Federal University of Bahia, Brazil
Goetz Botterweck   University of Limerick, Ireland
George Angelos Papadopoulos   University of Cyprus, Cyprus
Nan Niu   University of Cincinnati, USA
Oliver Hummel   University of Applied Sciences Mannheim,
                                  Germany
Hanen Hattab   Université du Québec à Montréal, Canada

Program Committee

Manel Abdellatif   University of Ottawa, Canada
Eduardo Almeida   Federal University of Bahia, Brazil
Apostolos Ampatzoglou   University of Macedonia, Greece
Francesca Arcelli Fontana   University of Milano-Bicocca, Italy
Claudia P. Ayala   Universitat Politècnica de Catalunya, Spain
Olivier Barais   IRISA, Inria, University of Rennes 1, France
Sihem Ben Sassi   University of Manouba, Tunisia
Djamal Benslimane   Université Claude Bernard Lyon 1, France
Mireille Blay-Fornarino   Université Côte d'Azur, CNRS, France
Jan Bosch   Chalmers University of Technology, Sweden
Rafael Capilla   Universidad Rey Juan Carlos, Spain
Stephanie Challita   Inria, France

Alexander Chatzigeorgiou	University of Macedonia, Greece
Coen De Roover	Vrije Universiteit Brussel, Belgium
Serge Demeyer	Universiteit Antwerpen, Belgium
Stéphane Ducasse	Inria, France
Laurence Duchien	University of Lille, France
Ghizlane El Boussaidi	École de technologie supérieure, Canada
John Favaro	Intecs, USA
Lidia Fuentes	University of Málaga, Spain
Jessie Galasso	University of Montréal, Canada
Barbara Gallina	Mälardalen University, Sweden
Iris Groher	Johannes Kepler University Linz, Austria
Andre Hora	Universidade Federal de Minas Gerais, Brazil
José Miguel Horcas Aguilera	University of Málaga, Spain
Marouane Kessentini	Oakland University, USA
Raula Gaikovina Kula	Nara Institute of Science and Technology, Japan
Lamia Labed Jilani	ISG Tunis, Tunisia
Tommi Mikkonen	University of Helsinki, Finland
Hafedh Mili	Université du Québec à Montréal, Canada
Raffaela Mirandola	Politecnico di Milano, Italy
Naouel Moha	École de technologie supérieure – Université du Québec, Canada
Nan Niu	University of Cincinnati, USA
Mourad Oussalah	LINA, University of Nantes, France
Quentin Perez	EuroMov DHM, University of Montpellier and IMT Mines Alès, France
Gilles Perrouin	University of Namur, Belgium
Gordana Rakic	University of Novi Sad, Serbia
Iris Reinhartz-Berger	University of Haifa, Israel
Houari Sahraoui	University of Montreal, Canada
Klaus Schmid	University of Hildesheim, Germany
Bedir Tekinerdogan	Wageningen University, The Netherlands
Paul Temple	University of Namur, Belgium
Xhevahire Ternava	Université de Rennes 1, France
Chouki Tibermacine	Université de Montpellier, France
Christelle Urtado	IMT Mines Alès, France
Christina von Flach	Federal University of Bahia, Brazil
Uwe Zdun	University of Vienna, Austria
Wei Zhang	Peking University, China
Tewfik Ziadi	Sorbonne University, France

Additional Reviewers

Acher, Mathieu
Ait Oubelli, Lynda
Della Vedova, Gianluca
Fortz, Sophie
Gasmallah, Noureddine

Hernández López, José Antonio
Islam, Syful
Saadi, Abdelfetah
Weyssow, Martin
Zaitsev, Oleksander

Contents

Code Recommendation and Reuse

Fine-Grained Analysis of Similar Code Snippets

Jessie Galasso(✉), Michalis Famelis, and Houari Sahraoui

Université de Montréal, DIRO, Montreal, Canada
{jessie.galasso-carbonnel,michalis.famelis,houari.sahraoui}@umontreal.ca

Abstract. Code recommendation aims to help programmers in their coding endeavors by suggesting appropriate code snippets to complete their program. Code recommendation approaches such as code search or code repair may rely on code snippets or code templates extracted from existing projects to provide these suggestions. In this context, extracting and characterizing reusable and recurring code structures beforehand is thus essential. In this paper, we characterize recurring code structures through parametrizable code templates. Code templates can outline the common structure in code snippets along with their variation points, hence providing a convenient way to define their structural similarity. Pattern Structure is a mathematical data analysis framework for organizing objects depending on their similarity: it produces a structure supporting clustering, analysis, and knowledge discovery tasks. We propose an approach leveraging this framework and similarity defined through code templates to highlight and organize groups of similar snippets. The produced structure contains all relevant code templates as well as refinement relationships between them, and can be used to support both manual and automated analysis. We present a case study where we apply this approach to analyze snippets for the task of code sophistication, which consists of identifying and suggesting missing conditional paths in programs.

Keywords: Code recommendation · Code template · Code similarity

1 Introduction

Code recommendation covers a set of tasks aiming at suggesting relevant code snippets to programmers to assist their coding endeavors. It includes suggesting the most likely next tokens (code auto-completion [9]), patches to fix a defect (automated program repair [13]) or examples of similar snippets to the one under development (code search [10]). Even though they do not share the same goal nor use the same approaches, these tasks have in common to rely on existing code bases to extract reusable knowledge about which code snippets to suggest and when. Some approaches, notably in code search and program repair, are founded on the reuse of code snippets or more generic code structures (i.e., abstract representations of the code) identified beforehand to perform their recommendations.

© Springer Nature Switzerland AG 2022
G. Perrouin et al. (Eds.): ICSR 2022, LNCS 13297, pp. 3–21, 2022.
https://doi.org/10.1007/978-3-031-08129-3_1

In this paper, we address the problem of characterizing and extracting the recurring structures in a set of code snippets (e.g., Listing 1.1) to foster reuse for code recommendation approaches. We use parametrizable code templates [5] as a mean to characterize recurring code structures. A code template is a code snippet with placeholders (missing code parts), which can be replaced with concrete values to instantiate a concrete code snippet. In other words, it is a parametrizable code snippet, representing all concrete code snippets which could be instantiated from it. We show how templates can serve as a mean to formalize structural similarity between snippets by outlining their common code parts along with their variation points. For instance, Fig. 2 (right-hand side) presents a template with one placeholder denoted $\langle ? \rangle$. Replacing $\langle ? \rangle$ by 0 leads to the snippet S_1 in Listing 1.1, and by `None` leads to S_2: this template thus outlines a common structure between these two snippets. Templates are widely used to capture code idioms to be reused by programmers in IDEs [11].

We propose an approach to assist developers in identifying important code templates to characterize recurring code structures in a given set of code snippets. This approach relies on Pattern Structure [7], a data analysis framework for knowledge extraction and representation. Following the framework, we first create clusters of code snippets sharing structural properties, and characterize each cluster with a template representing the structural similarity of its contents. Then, we organize these clusters in a hierarchy which reflects relations of specialization and generalization between templates. The obtained hierarchical structure naturally emphasizes what is common and what varies between clusters of similar code snippets, at several levels of increasing detail, which enables fine-grained analysis of recurring code structures. Pattern Structure guarantees that we uncover all relevant templates in the considered set of snippets and organizes them in a way that support exploration and knowledge discovery. We implemented a prototype to extract and browse the relevant templates of a given set of fragments. We present a case study about analyzing snippets for code sophistication, a code recommendation task aiming at suggesting missing behaviors in a program.

This paper is organized as follows. We discuss the characterization of similar code snippets with templates in Sect. 2. Section 3 shows how to leverage these templates to produce a hierarchical clustering of similar snippets with Pattern Structure. In Sect. 4, we discuss how the properties of this hierarchical structure are useful for analyzing and reusing code templates, and present four use cases. Section 5 presents the results of applying this approach on sophistication snippets to detect recurring code structures in missing conditional paths. Related work is presented in Sect. 6 and Sect. 7 concludes this paper.

(S_1)

```
1   if len(x) == 0:
2       return 0
```

(S_2)

```
1   if len(x) == 0:
2       return None
```

(S_3)

```
1   if len(x) == 0:
2       continue
```

(S_4)

```
1   if len(x) == 0:
2       return y.values[0]
```

(S_5)

```
1   if x.values[0] == 0:
2       return None
```

Listing 1.1. Similar code snippets

2 Characterizing Similar Code Snippets with Templates

To motivate our approach, in Listing 1.1 we introduce 5 snippets corresponding to conditional paths written in Python. Figure 1 shows their corresponding abstract syntax trees (ASTs). All 5 snippets share a common structure, i.e., a conditional check, followed by a return statement, but differ on the checked condition and the return value.

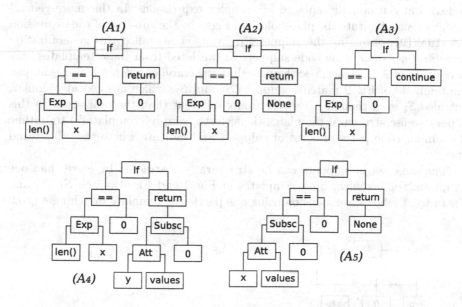

Fig. 1. Simplified ASTs of the code snippets from Listing 1.1

2.1   Structural Code Templates

A code template is a code snippet with *"holes"* or *placeholders* that usually replace identifiers (class, method or variable names) or literals [5]. Replacing the placeholders of a template by concrete values generates a concrete code snippet. We say that the obtained snippet *instantiates* the template, or that the template *matches* the snippet. Placeholders can eventually be typed to restrict the values which can replace them.

Code snippets which only differ in their identifiers and literals are said to be *lexically similar*. They possess the same AST structure but may differ at the leaf nodes. For instance, snippets S_1 and S_2 (Listing 1.1) are lexically similar: their corresponding ASTs A_1 and A_2 have the same structure (i.e., the same internal nodes) and only the leaves under their `return` node differ. A template thus has an AST in which at least one leaf is a special placeholder node. Templates are lexical abstractions of all code snippets that have the same structure but have different identifiers and literals. Such templates are called *lexical templates*. Figure 2 shows a template with one placeholder (denoted ⟨?⟩) that is a lexical abstraction of snippets S_1 and S_2: if we replace the placeholder by 0 we obtain S_1, and by None we obtain S_2.

Evans et al. [5] generalized lexical abstractions such that template placeholders may replace not only a leaf but any sub-tree of the AST. Placeholders then still correspond to leaves in the AST of the template (they cannot be internal nodes), but can now be replaced by complex expressions. In this more general case, we can substitute the placeholder in Fig. 2 by the sub-tree of the expression `y.values[0]`, obtaining the snippet S_4. Evans et al. called this generalization *structural abstraction*, as code snippets instantiated from these templates may have different AST structures: they are thus *structural templates*. In our example, the template of Fig. 2 matches snippets S_1 and S_2, which are lexically similar, but also S_4 even though it is structurally different than the other two. In this paper, we use structural templates (henceforth, simply "templates") to outline the similar code parts of a set of snippets and indicate where they differ and how.

The same set of snippets can be structurally abstracted by more than one template. For instance, both templates of Fig. 2 and Fig. 3 match S_1, S_2 and S_4. In what follows, we focus on using one particular template matching a given

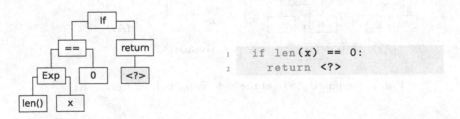

Fig. 2. Template with one placeholder, representing a conditional check and a return statement

set of snippets, which is the one characterizing their maximal similarity (i.e., the least abstract template) with the smallest number of variation points (i.e., placeholders). We call it the *common template* of the set of snippets. The AST of the common template corresponds to the largest common AST of the considered snippets, with the smaller number of placeholders needed to instantiate these snippets.

Definition 1 (Common template AST). *The common template AST of a given set of ASTs corresponds to the AST containing all nodes whose root path (path between the node and the root) are present in all given ASTs. The common template AST also contains placeholders indicating the first occurrence of a different node in a downward path from the root to the leaves.*

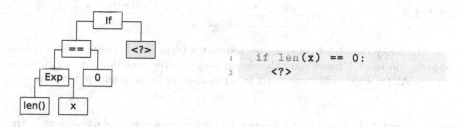

Fig. 3. Template with one placeholder, representing a conditional check

The common template can be computed by performing simultaneous tree traversals of the ASTs: if the nodes are equivalent, it is kept in the AST of the common template, otherwise it is replaced by a placeholder. The template of Fig. 3 does not represent the common template of $\{S_1, S_2, S_4\}$, because the `return` node that is common to the three corresponding ASTs is not included in the template. Rather, their common template is the one presented in Fig. 2. On the other hand, the template in Fig. 3 is the common template of the set $\{S_1, S_2, S_3, S_4\}$, given that S_3 does not have a `return` node.

The common template of a set of snippets characterizes their similarity in terms of their shared AST structure. The size of the common template may hint at how similar the snippets are: the bigger the common template, the more structural similarity they share. In the basic case where we have two or more syntactically equivalent snippets, the common template is a template without placeholders, that cannot be instantiated, i.e., a snippet.

2.2 Similarity Between Templates

As templates are generalized ASTs that can potentially have special leaf nodes to represent placeholders, we can extend to them the notion of similarity based on common AST nodes. Following Definition 1, given a set of templates, we can extract a common template. We show the ASTs of two templates and their

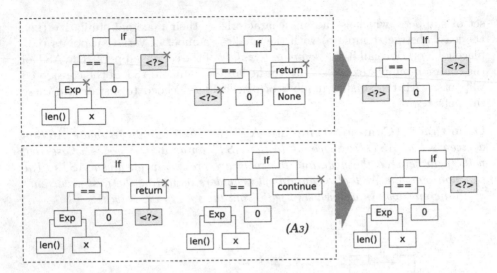

Fig. 4. Similarity templates between two templates (top) and between a snippet and a template (bottom). Crosses show the closest nodes to the root that are not common in the two ASTs, which will correspond to a placeholder in the common template.

common template in Fig. 4 (top). Divergent nodes, yielding to placeholders in the common template, are marked in the figure with an X. Extraction of common templates can also be applied to mixed sets that contain both templates and snippets. We show in Fig. 4 (bottom) the similarity template extracted between A_3 (the AST of snippet S_3) and the template of Fig. 2.

We explained previously that snippets can be instantiated from their common template by replacing a placeholder with a concrete AST sub-tree. In a similar way, a template can be instantiated from another template by *specializing* a placeholder, i.e., replacing it by a sub-tree which may itself contain placeholders. This operation amounts to template *refinement*. Instantiating a concrete code snippet from a template can thus be seen as a process of step-wise template refinement, each step further specializing a placeholder until all placeholders are replaced by concrete code.

Next, we present a mathematical framework which leverages common templates and template refinement to organize snippets and templates by similarity. We then show how to use it for fine-grained analysis and extraction of recurring code structures.

3   Structuring Templates by Similarity with Pattern Structure

Pattern Structure [7] is a structural framework for data analysis and knowledge discovery and representation of a set of *objects* characterized by *descriptions*. It enables building canonical hierarchies of specialization which organize objects depending on the *similarity* of their descriptions. In this section, we present the key definitions of this framework, and show how we apply it to organize templates by similarity.

3.1 Input

As input, the framework considers a triple $(O, (D, \sqcap), \delta)$, where O is a finite set of objects, D is a set of descriptions and $\delta: O \to D$ maps each object to its description. The set of descriptions in D can be of any type and must be associated with a *similarity operation* (denoted $\sqcap$). When applied on a set of descriptions from D, this similarity operation must return another description from D representing the similarity, or generalization of its arguments. The similarity operation is idempotent, commutative and associative, and is associated with a subsumption relation $\sqsubseteq$ providing the descriptions in D with a specialization/generalization order:

$$\forall d_1, d_2 \in D, d_1 \sqsubseteq d_2 \Leftrightarrow d_1 \sqcap d_2 = d_1$$

Thus, $(D, \sqcap)$ forms a meet-semilattice, i.e., a structure in which each subset of descriptions from D has an upper bound, namely the element in D that describes their similarity.

In this paper, we consider that the objects in O are code snippets (e.g., the one in Listing 1.1). As objects' descriptions, we consider their ASTs: D thus includes the ASTs of the snippets in O (without placeholders, as in Fig. 1) and δ maps the snippets in O to their corresponding ASTs in D. Based on the definitions above, the extraction of the common template AST from a set of ASTs corresponds to the similarity operation $\sqcap$. Thus, the set of descriptions D includes *(i)* the ASTs of the snippets in O and *(ii)* all the common template ASTs that can be computed from them. For instance, if the snippets in O are the ones from Listing 1.1, then A_2 and A_3 are included in D. Their similarity $(A_2 \sqcap A_3)$ is characterized by the AST $A_{2,3}$ (corresponding to Fig. 3), which is thus also in D. In this way, $(D, \sqcap)$ forms a meet-semilattice, in which each subset of ASTs has an upper-bound, namely the AST characterizing their structural similarity. Figure 5 shows an example meet-semilattice based on the three ASTs A_2, A_3 and A_5.

The subsumption relation associated with this similarity operation here organizes the ASTs in D by specialization/generalization: if $A_2 \sqcap A_3 = A_{2,3}$, then $A_{2,3} \sqsubseteq A_2$ and $A_{2,3} \sqsubseteq A_3$. It corresponds to the notion of template refinement discussed in Sect. 2.2: $A_{2,3}$ is a more generic template than A_2 and A_3, and thus A_2 and A_3 can be instantiated from $A_{2,3}$. In Fig. 5, an edge between two ASTs shows the subsumption relation: a template subsumes another template if it can be instantiated from it. The higher a template is placed in the hierarchy, the more abstract it is (i.e., the fewer concrete nodes it has). In Fig. 5, the template of level 3 (top) represents the similarity of the templates of level 2, and corresponds to the common template of the ASTs of level 1 (bottom).

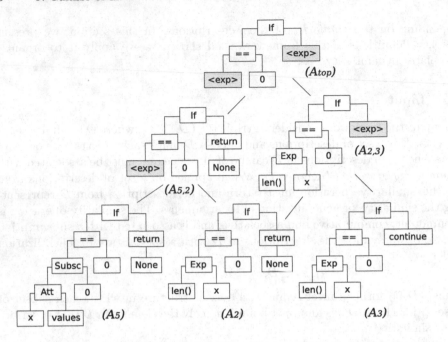

Fig. 5. Excerpt of meet-semilattice of templates. The lowest upper bound of any subset of elements shows their common template

3.2 Building Process

Pattern Concepts. Given a triple $(O, (D, \sqcap), \delta)$, the framework first extracts a finite set of *pattern concepts*, denoted C_K. The extraction process relies on two derivation operators: $\alpha : 2^O \mapsto D$ and $\beta : D \mapsto 2^O$. The operator α associates with a subset of objects $O' \in O$ the most specific description of $(D, \sqcap)$ matching all objects of O':

$$\alpha(O') = \bigsqcap_{o \in O'} \delta(o), \text{ with } O' \in O$$

The operator β associates each description $d \in (D, \sqcap)$ with all objects from O matching this description:

$$\beta(d) = \{o \in O \mid d \sqsubseteq \delta(o)\}, \text{ with } d \in (D, \sqcap)$$

A pattern concept is a pair (O', d), $O' \in O$, $d \in (D, \sqcap)$, such that $\alpha(O') = d$ and $\beta(d) = O'$. C_K is obtained by applying these two operators on all subsets of O. Each pattern concept represents a maximal group that guarantees that the description d is the most specialized description that describes a given set of objects O', and that there are no objects outside O' that are described by d.

In our example, a pattern concept takes the form of a group of snippets associated with a template. The operator α associates with a set of snippets O' the common template of their ASTs. For instance, $\alpha(\{S_1, S_2, S_3\}) = A_{1,2,3,4}$,

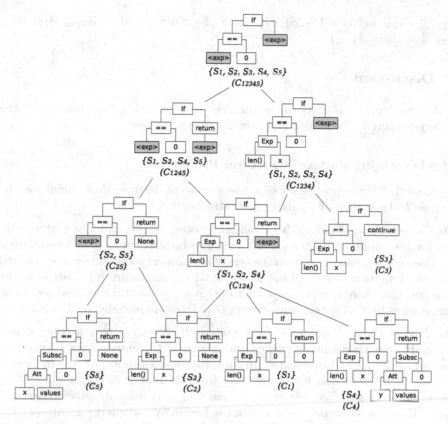

Fig. 6. Pattern concept lattice based on common templates (the bottom concept is omitted because it does not provide any useful information)

where $A_{1,2,3,4}$ is the template presented in Fig. 3. The operator β associates a template d with all snippets matching it. Thus, $\beta(A_{1,2,3,4}) = \{S_1, S_2, S_3, S_4\}$. The pair $(\{S_1, S_2, S_3, S_4\}, A_{1,2,3,4})$ is thus a pattern concept, shown as C_{1234} in Fig. 6. From the five snippets of Listing 1.1, a total of 11 pattern concepts can be extracted: Fig. 6 shows 10 of them and omits the trivial pattern concept representing the empty set of snippets.

Specialization Order. Finally, the framework provides the set of pattern concepts C_K with a partial order $\leq$. This order is based on the subsumption relation $\sqsubseteq$ which exists between the descriptions of each pattern concept. Given two concepts $C_a = (O_a, d_a)$ and $C_b = (O_b, d_b)$, $C_a \leq C_b$ iff $O_a \subseteq O_b$ and $d_b \sqsubseteq d_a$. C_a is then called a sub-concept of C_b, and C_b a super-concept of C_a. The set of concepts provided with the partial order forms a lattice structure $(C_K, \leq)$ organizing the concepts in a specialization hierarchy.

In Fig. 6, the specialization order is represented by the edges. If $A_{1,2,4}$ is the template from Fig. 2 that corresponds to the concept C_{124} in Fig. 6, then

$C_{124} \leq C_{1234}$ because $\{S_1, S_2, S_4\} \subseteq \{S_1, S_2, S_3, S_4\}$ and $A_{1234} \sqsubseteq A_{124}$ (i.e., A_{124} specializes A_{1234}).

4 Discussion

In this section, we discuss the advantages of structuring templates with the Pattern Structure framework and present some use cases.

4.1 Leveraging Pattern Structures Properties

We identified three properties of pattern concept lattices that useful for the analysis and selection of recurring code structures.

The Pattern Concept Lattice Is Canonical. In other words, only one pattern concept lattice can be built for a given input. The building process is deterministic and does not depend on any parameters. This property guarantees a sound and complete template identification: all maximal templates are represented in the concepts, and there is no concept that does not represent a maximal template. This ensures that all potentially relevant templates are included in the structure.

The Partial Order Provides a Specialization Hierarchy. Given a concept and the template it represents, its super-concepts show the more abstract templates from which it can be instantiated. In turn, its sub-concepts show the more specific templates that can be instantiated from it. In Fig. 6, C_{25}, C_{124} and C_2 are examples of sub-concepts of C_{1245}, and C_{12345} is the only super-concept of C_{1245}. Thus, the concepts at the top of the hierarchy cover large groups of snippets characterized by generic templates. Going down the hierarchy reveals more specific templates corresponding to smaller groups of snippets. The structure depicts the templates of subsets of snippets at different level of granularity, thus enabling to explore recurring templates at increasing levels of detail.

The Neighborhood of a Concept Shows Its Most Similar Concepts. The direct sub-concepts of a given concept show the most similar descriptions which are a refinement of its description. While its sub-concepts represent all possible refinements of its associated template, the direct sub-concepts show the possible *minimal* refinements. In our example, the two direct sub-concepts of C_{1245} are C_{25} and C_{124}. C_5 is also its sub-concept but not a direct one. C_{25}, C_{124} and C_5 can therefore all be instantiated from C_{1245}, but only C_{25} and C_{124} are minimal specializations. C_5 is not a minimal specialization as it requires two specialization steps from C_{1245} (first to C_{25} and then to C_5). The same logic applies for the direct super-concepts: we can explore the closest generalizations of a given template by inspecting the direct super-concepts of its concept. This enables the stepwise exploration of the specializations of a template with only minimal steps. In other words, following a chain from top to bottom corresponds to a stepwise template refinement process. Concepts with the most sub-concepts (generally situated at the top of the lattice structure) are interesting for finding reusable and recurring code structures as they show the predominant recurring templates, i.e., the ones shared by the more snippets. If a template is too abstract to be relevant for reuse, we can analyze the templates of its direct sub-concepts, because they show a way to divide the current group of similar snippets in smaller yet cohesive groups.

4.2 Use Cases

Below we describe how the concept lattice can be used to improve code recommendation.

Extracting Templates. Concepts that represent maximal groups of similar snippets and their associated template provide a strong foundation to identify recurring code structures. The pattern concept lattice shows templates' occurrences in a given set of code snippets. This can help define fine-grained metrics to filter a large set and alleviate the effort of manual analysis. The identified templates can be used to better understand recurring code structures in a code base and to define reusable and parametrizable templates. They can help find coding idioms in a given project, or find recurring structures across projects (e.g., API usages).

Exploring the Space of Templates. Exploratory search [16] is an information retrieval strategy aimed at guiding a user into progressively discovering a set of documents by navigating (or browsing) into a structured space of these documents. Conceptual structures are an advantageous support for exploration [8], notably because the direct neighbors of a concept represent concepts with the most similar descriptions and thus guarantee an exploration process with minimal steps. In our case, it enables navigating from one maximal relevant template to another by following their specialization/generalization relations. This could help discovery and analysis of templates through exploration.

Supporting Code Recommendation. This way of organizing templates can help improve code completion and code search approaches. Code completion seeks to predict the next tokens a programmer would write at a specific location in the code being written. Recent work targets complex suggestions such as sequences of tokens [9], or even structured code snippets such as API usages [20]. Code search is the task of finding code examples to help the developer implement what they have in mind. Code search approaches usually rely on information retrieval to find in a code database those snippets that correspond to a query; the query is either formulated by the programmer or inferred automatically from the code under development [10]. Our proposed structuring of code templates can help both these tasks. These templates could be used to help assess the pertinence of suggested code, or to recommend similar snippets to the suggested one. We also envision suggesting not only fully formed snippets but relevant also parametrizable templates directly to the programmer. In this case, structured templates could help suggest potential refinements, or help the programmer explore a space of similar and relevant templates. In code search, queried snippets could be reorganized by similarity to simplify the output presented to the user by grouping similar snippets.

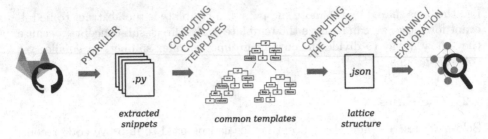

Fig. 7. Process to support the identification of recurring code templates

5 Case Study: Reusable Templates for Code Sophistication

Behavioral program analysis considers a program mainly as a collection of behaviors, i.e., sets of actions to be performed under certain conditions. Each behavior is an execution path for a given scenario (i.e., combination of input values) that is enabled by path conditions in the body of the program. Unusual combinations of input values may correspond to atypical scenarios which need to be handled by special conditional paths. However, developers are prone to omit such atypical scenarios from specification documents: missing conditional paths are known to be hard to detect [3] and are one of the largest source of bugs [22]. *Code sophistication* [6] is a type of code recommendation that suggests missing conditional paths in the form of *if*-blocks to handle these atypical scenarios. Previous work on missing conditional paths suggests that they recurrently address some typical behavior scenarios, such as error handling, variable assignments, or early returns. In order to produce good sophistication recommendations, we need to better understand and characterize the kinds of conditional paths that are usually missing. We thus focus on code commits where developers added *if*-blocks to add some previously missing behavior corresponding to an unaddressed scenario. By analyzing recurring code structures in such added *if*-blocks, we can better understand and characterize what the kinds of conditional paths that are usually missing from programs and thus produce better sophistication recommendations.

In this section we try to answer the question: *How can the pattern structure be used to comprehensively explore a set of snippets and identify relevant templates?* We present how we applied our approach to discover and explore recurring code templates in code snippets that represent missing conditional paths. The process is shown in Fig. 7. First we extracted a dataset by gathering code snippets that represent missing conditional paths (Sect. 5.1). Then, we computed common templates and the lattice structure (Sect. 5.2) based on the extracted snippets. Finally, we show how to support the identification of relevant recurring templates (Section 5.3). This is the first step towards building code recommendation tools for code sophistication.

5.1   Dataset

The version history of programs can reveal valuable insights about how programmers address defects in programs. We decided to focus on commits where a developer added conditional paths (*if*-blocks) to the code. Such a code change indicates that the pre-existing code version omitted some important conditional path which the developer tried to include by adding the missing behaviour [22].

We analyzed the version histories of 290 Git repositories from GitHub and GitLab. We used the advanced search of both platforms to select repositories containing code written in Python. We prioritized projects with large commit histories (>1000) but also included trending projects even if they have fewer commits. We then used PyDriller [23] to collect and analyze all the commits of a given repository and find changes in methods according to the following criteria: *a)* no code is deleted by the commit, *b)* the added lines are consecutive (a single snippet is added), and *c)* the added snippet corresponds to an `if` block. This filtering approach allows us to identify changes that focus on adding an *if*-block in a method. For each changed method, we isolated the code snippet added by the commit and stored it in a file. In total, we analyzed more than 2 million commits and extracted 25 000 methods where a conditional path was added by a developer. The added conditional paths amounted to between 1 and 75 lines of code, with an average of 1.9 lines per snippet (plus 1 line with the *if* statement and the condition). The snippets in Listing 1.1 were inspired from snippets in this dataset.

5.2   Implementation

We then apply the proposed approach on the extracted *if*-blocks to characterize recurring code structures in missing conditional paths. We implemented a two-step procedure. First, we compute the common template of a given set of ASTs. Then, we compute the lattice structure by relying on the common template extraction.

Computing the Common Templates. We used the AST Python library[1] to build the AST of each code snippet. This library provides a parser and an implementation of the Visitor design pattern for handling the nodes of an AST. So, starting from the root node, we traverse pairs of ASTs in parallel to build a third AST that represents their common template. If two nodes have the same type and the same values, we add a copy of them to the common AST and continue with the children nodes. If two nodes are of the same type but have different values (e.g., they are both binary operations, albeit different ones), we add to the common AST a node of this type but with no values (in this case, an empty node of type AST.BinOp). If the two nodes are of different types, we add to the AST an empty node representing an expression. In the two last cases, we interrupt the traversal and do not visit the children nodes of the divergent nodes. The empty nodes act as placeholders ("holes") and correspond to the

---

[1] https://docs.python.org/3/library/ast.html

most specific type that characterizes the two divergent nodes. This produces a common template AST that can itself be traversed during the computation of subsequent template ASTs.

Computing the Lattice Structure. To extract the maximal templates, we applied the common template extraction on all code snippets in the dataset. After computing the AST of each snippet, we obtained 17 166 unique ASTs, meaning that a third of the extracted snippets were syntactically equivalent. Our method first computes the common ASTs of each pair of these initial ASTs. Then, it computes the common ASTs of each pair of the common ASTs produced in the previous step. This repeats until no new AST is created. After computing the similarity between the initial 17 166 ASTs, we obtained 52 241 new ASTs corresponding to templates. In the next iteration, we generated 8 421 more ASTs, and in the next, 5 more ASTs. After this fourth iteration, no new AST was generated. During this process, we kept track of which pairs of ASTs generated which templates. In this way, we are able to infer the specialization relationships and thus the partial order between templates associated with the obtained ASTs. We stored all ASTs, the related snippets and the partial order in a JSON file.

One disadvantage of Pattern Structures is the size of the structure and the cost involved in its computation. For a triple $(O, (D, \sqcap), \delta)$, the associated lattice structure may have a number of concepts up to $2^{min(|O|,|D|)}$, even though it rarely reaches this upper-bound. In our case study, we obtained a total of 77 828 concepts for both the concrete code snippets and the extracted templates. However, not all templates are of interest, especially for our application scenario, where the aim is to focus on the ones representing recurring structures. As discussed earlier, such templates are usually situated at the top of the structure. This allows pruning the structure to reduce its size. For instance, in the presented study, if we choose to include only templates matching at least 200 snippets from the original dataset, we obtain a more manageable structure of 211 concepts. The cost of the lattice computation can be significant, especially in our case, as similarity is computed by tree comparison. With small optimizations, our implementation took about 5 h to generate the structure from the 25 000 snippets. Further optimizing the generation process is an interesting avenue for future work.

5.3   Analysis by Exploration

As described in the previous section, we can prune the structure to only include templates representing many snippets, and perform a manual analysis on this smaller number of templates. However, without leveraging the refinement relations between the templates, this manual analysis would be tedious and error prone. To enable a step by step analysis of the space of templates, we implemented a GUI prototype[2] to perform exploratory search based on the structure stored in the JSON file created in Sect. 5.2. We show screenshots of the navigation interface in Fig. 8.

---

[2] https://github.com/jgalasso/structural-template-lattice.

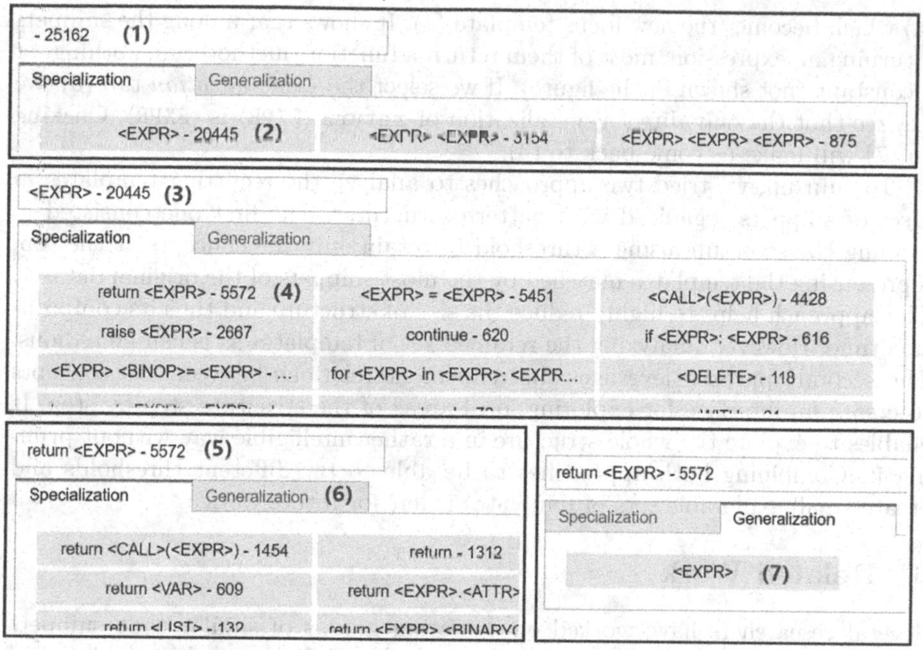

Fig. 8. Screenshots of the navigation interface

Given a template on which we want to focus as the basis for exploration (the "focus template"), the interface can display its direct generalizations and direct specializations. The focus template is displayed in the box at the top (e.g., 1, 3 and 5). Below we show two tabs: one for its direct template specializations, and the other for its generalizations. Each tab shows a grid with buttons for the relevant templates. Clicking on a template button changes the focus template to the new template and updates the display to show its own generalizations and specializations. Each template is followed by a number representing its occurrence. In Fig. 8 (4), "return ⟨EXPR⟩ - 5 572" states that 5 572 concrete code snippets of the dataset match the template "return ⟨EXPR⟩".

The navigation starts with the common template of all snippets, which in our study happened to be empty. Figure 8 (1) shows the empty template being the focus template, which is matched by all of the 25 162 snippets. Snippets with different numbers of lines are not comparable with the current state of the approach, so the direct specializations tab of the empty template shows groups of snippets depending on their number of lines. We can see that out of 25 162 snippets, 20 445 have one line (they match the template "⟨EXPR⟩"), 3 154 have two lines and 875 have three. If we click on the template representing all snippets with one line (2), it becomes the focus template (3). We can see now that most one-line snippets in the studied dataset return an expression, perform an assignment or call a function or a method. To know which kinds of expressions are returned the most, we can click on the corresponding template

(4) which becomes the new focus template (5). It shows that among the snippets returning an expression, most of them return a function/method call, nothing, or a constant (not shown in the figure). If we select the *Generalization* tab (6), we can see that the only direct generalization of return ⟨EXPR⟩ is ⟨EXPR⟩. Clicking on (7) will make us come back to (3).

To sum up, we tried two approaches to analyze the recurring templates in a set of snippets organized with pattern structures. The first one consisted in pruning the structure using a threshold to retain only the concepts at the top, representing the templates matched by the most snippets of the original dataset. This approach helps to highly reduce the size of structure and thus its computation time. However, analyzing the retained set of templates as is can be tedious. The second approach leverages the refinement relations between the concepts to create an interface for exploring local areas of the structure step by step. It enables to explore the whole structure in a rather intelligible way without pruning it. Combining both approaches to be able to try different thresholds and create small explorable sets of templates is left for future work.

6 Related Work

Several researchers have worked on detecting groups of similar code snippets based on their ASTs. Kontogiannis et al. [14] and Jiang et al. [12] identified clusters of similar snippets based on feature vectors of structural program features, including features based on the AST. Other methods focus on representing the ASTs as sequences to find recurring subsequences. Koschke et al. [15] proposed to linearize AST nodes by a preorder traversal to apply suffix tree clone detection. Suffix trees allow fast implementation of string search operations such as finding occurrences of patterns. Yang et al. [24] generated sequences from ASTs in which leaves were replaced by value types (lexical abstraction), and used the Smith-Waterman sequence alignment algorithm to compute similarity scores. Nichols et al. [21] proposed a hybrid approach combining a structural detection similar to the one of [24] and a nominal clone detection approach. Nominal clone detection is based on the idea that similar snippets will use similar identifiers. In comparison, our work relies on the AST structure to group similar snippets. Some authors work directly on the structure of ASTs. Merlo et al. [17] first identified different syntactic blocks (statements, methods, classes, etc.) and their inclusion relationships for the AST of a project. Then, they created clusters of similar blocks to detect higher level structural similarity. Baxter et al. [2] found similar snippets by detecting recurring exact sub-trees in ASTs. They checked the parents of sequences of exact sub-trees to detect near-miss clones. In our work, we do not consider similarity between sub-trees if their parents differ: in this way, the extracted templates keep a consistent code structure which can be refined. In [4], Chodarev et al. used a pattern recognition algorithm to detect lexical templates. Narasimhan et al. [19] proposed a method to merge similar snippets as part of a refactoring task. In comparison, we do not provide an implementation of the merged similar snippets, but a structure showing the possible paths of parametrization of the common parts of the similar snippets.

Other works used templates to characterize and manage similar snippets. Evans et al. [5] first generated candidate templates from the AST: for each node, they took the full sub-tree rooted in this node and replaced descendants at several levels of depth by placeholders. Then, they retained templates occurring at least twice and applied an operation called *pattern improvement* which computes the largest template matching all its occurrences. Contrary to their work, we do not identify potential patterns in an AST, but we rely on their definition of structural templates and pattern improvement to characterize similarity between a given set of snippets. We then extend these notions to identify the set of all maximal relevant templates of a set of snippets and structure them by refinement. In the context of code repair, Bader et al. [1] proposed an approach to extract recurring edit patterns in the form of pairs of ASTs representing the code before and after the repair. They generalized pairs of edit patterns by computing common templates of the associated ASTs and organize them in a hierarchy represented by a dendrogram. Contrary to our approach, their building process performs approximations to increase computation efficiency, and does not guarantee the identification of all maximal templates. Molderez et al. [18] addressed the problem of automatically generalizing or specializing a given template. They use a search-based approach relying on a set of concrete snippets which should be matched or not by the new template to identify a sequence of modifications to be applied on the current one. In our work, we organize all templates in a structure that emphasize all minimal modifications that need to be performed to obtain a template from another.

7 Conclusion and Future Work

We presented an approach for fine-grained analysis of the similarity of a set of snippets to support the identification and reuse of recurring code structures in the form of templates. We showed how templates can characterize the similarity of snippets, and how to produce a hierarchical clustering of similar snippets using the Pattern Structure framework. We applied this approach to detect relevant templates for code sophistication, and showed how the hierarchical structure we produced can support exploratory search to navigate the space of extracted templates.

In the future, we plan to investigate additional ways of capturing similarity. For example we could adapt the current similarity discovery operation between snippets to consider similarity between snippets that have different numbers of statements. We also want to improve the quality of extracted templates by pre-processing the snippets before assessing their similarity. We plan to extend our current approach to consider lexical information and improve the variability expressed by the extracted templates. Finally, we plan to evaluate different analysis approaches to determine the practicability of extracted templates for end-users.

References

1. Bader, J., Scott, A., Pradel, M., Chandra, S.: Getafix: learning to fix bugs automatically. Proc. ACM Program. Lang. **3**(OOPSLA), 1–27 (2019)
2. Baxter, I.D., Yahin, A., Moura, L., Sant'Anna, M., Bier, L.: Clone detection using abstract syntax trees. In: International Conference on Software Maintenance, pp. 368–377. IEEE (1998)
3. Chen, T.H., Nagappan, M., Shihab, E., Hassan, A.E.: An empirical study of dormant bugs. In: 11th Working Conference on Mining Software Repositories, pp. 82–91 (2014)
4. Chodarev, S., Pietriková, E., Kollár, J.: Haskell clone detection using pattern comparing algorithm. In: Intnational Conference on Engineering of Modern Electric Systems, pp. 1–4. IEEE (2015)
5. Evans, W.S., Fraser, C.W., Ma, F.: Clone detection via structural abstraction. Software Qual. J. **17**(4), 309–330 (2009)
6. Galasso, J., Famelis, M., Sahraoui, H.A.: Code sophistication: from code recommendation to logic recommendation. CoRR abs/2201.07674 (2022)
7. Ganter, B., Kuznetsov, S.O.: Pattern structures and their projections. In: Delugach, H.S., Stumme, G. (eds.) ICCS-ConceptStruct 2001. LNCS (LNAI), vol. 2120, pp. 129–142. Springer, Heidelberg (2001). https://doi.org/10.1007/3-540-44583-8_10
8. Godin, R., Pichet, C., Gecsei, J.: Design of a browsing interface for information retrieval. In: International Conference on Research and Development in Information Retrieval, pp. 32–39 (1989)
9. Hindle, A., Barr, E.T., Gabel, M., Su, Z., Devanbu, P.: On the naturalness of software. Commun. ACM **59**(5), 122–131 (2016)
10. Holmes, R., Murphy, G.C.: Using structural context to recommend source code examples. In: 27th International Conference on Software Engineering, pp. 117–125 (2005)
11. Jacob, F., Tairas, R.: Code template inference using language models. In: Proceedings of the 48th Annual Southeast Regional Conference, pp. 1–6 (2010)
12. Jiang, L., Misherghi, G., Su, Z., Glondu, S.: Deckard: scalable and accurate tree-based detection of code clones. In: International Conference on Software Engineering, pp. 96–105. IEEE (2007)
13. Kim, D., Nam, J., Song, J., Kim, S.: Automatic patch generation learned from human-written patches. In: International Conference on Software Engineering, pp. 802–811. IEEE (2013)
14. Kontogiannis, K.A., DeMori, R., Merlo, E., Galler, M., Bernstein, M.: Pattern matching for clone and concept detection. Autom. Softw. Eng. **3**(1), 77–108 (1996)
15. Koschke, R., Falke, R., Frenzel, P.: Clone detection using abstract syntax suffix trees. In: 2006 13th Working Conference on Reverse Engineering, pp. 253–262. IEEE (2006)
16. Marchionini, G.: Exploratory search: from finding to understanding. Commun. ACM **49**(4), 41–46 (2006)
17. Merlo, E., Lavoie, T.: Computing structural types of clone syntactic blocks. In: 2009 16th Working Conference on Reverse Engineering, pp. 274–278. IEEE (2009)
18. Molderez, T., De Roover, C.: Search-based generalization and refinement of code templates. In: Sarro, F., Deb, K. (eds.) SSBSE 2016. LNCS, vol. 9962, pp. 192–208. Springer, Cham (2016). https://doi.org/10.1007/978-3-319-47106-8_13

19. Narasimhan, K.: Clone merge-an eclipse plugin to abstract near-clone C++ methods. In: IEEE/ACM International Conference on Automated Software Engineering, pp. 819–823. IEEE (2015)
20. Nguyen, A.T., Nguyen, T.N.: Graph-based statistical language model for code. In: 37th International Conference on Software Engineering, vol. 1, pp. 858–868. IEEE (2015)
21. Nichols, L., Emre, M., Hardekopf, B.: Structural and nominal cross-language clone detection. In: International Conference on Fundamental Approaches to Software Engineering, pp. 247–263 (2019)
22. Raghavan, S., Rohana, R., Leon, D., Podgurski, A., Augustine, V.: Dex: a semantic-graph differencing tool for studying changes in large code bases. In: 20th International Conference on Software Maintenance, pp. 188–197. IEEE (2004)
23. Spadini, D., Aniche, M., Bacchelli, A.: PyDriller: Python framework for mining software repositories (2018). https://doi.org/10.1145/3236024.3264598
24. Yang, Y., Ren, Z., Chen, X., Jiang, H.: Structural function based code clone detection using a new hybrid technique. In: Annual Computer Software and Applications Conference (COMPSAC), vol. 1, pp. 286–291. IEEE (2018)

DepMiner: Automatic Recommendation of Transformation Rules for Method Deprecation

Oleksandr Zaitsev[1,2]([✉]), Stéphane Ducasse[2], Nicolas Anquetil[2], and Arnaud Thiefaine[1]

[1] Arolla, Paris, France
{oleksandr.zaitsev,arnaud.thiefaine}@arolla.fr
[2] Inria, Univ. Lille, CNRS, Centrale Lille, UMR 9189 - CRIStAL, Lille, France
{stephane.ducasse,nicolas.anquetil}@inria.fr
https://www.arolla.fr , https://www.inria.fr

Abstract. Software applications often depend on external libraries and must be updated when one of those libraries releases a new version. To make this process easier, library developers try to reduce the negative effect of breaking changes by deprecating the API elements before removing them and suggesting replacements to the clients. Modern programming languages and IDEs provide powerful tools for deprecations that can reference the replacement or incorporate the rules written by library developers and use them to automatically update the client code. However, in practice library developers often miss the deprecation opportunities and fail to document the deprecations. In this work, we propose to help library developers support their clients with better deprecations. We rely on the transforming deprecations offered by Pharo and use data mining to detect the missing deprecation opportunities and generate the transformation rules. We implemented our approach for Pharo in a prototype tool called *DepMiner*. We have applied our tool to five open-source projects and proposed the generated deprecations to core developers of those projects. 63 recommended deprecations were accepted as pull requests.

1 Introduction

Most modern software depends on multiple external libraries [3]. Each one of those libraries is a separate project that is managed by its own team of developers. Like any other software, libraries evolve from one version to another, parts of their Application Programming Interfaces (API) are changed (classes, methods, or fields get renamed, deleted, or moved around, new functionalities are introduced, etc. [12]). As a result, developers depending on those libraries must either update their code or continue having outdated and no longer maintained dependencies.

This work was financed by the Arolla software company.

G. Perrouin et al. (Eds.): ICSR 2022, LNCS 13297, pp. 22–37, 2022.
https://doi.org/10.1007/978-3-031-08129-3_2

Deprecation is a common practice for supporting library evolution by notifying client systems about the changed or removed features and helping them adapt to the new API. Instead of removing a feature in release n, it is marked as *deprecated* (*"to be removed"*) and only actually removed in a later release $n + k$. Client systems that call a deprecated feature receive a deprecation warning which gives developers time to update their code.

It is a good practice for library developers to supply deprecations with code comments or warning messages that suggest a replacement for an obsolete item. For example, *"Method a() is deprecated, use b() instead"*. To support this practice, Java provides the @Deprecated annotation as well as the @deprecated Javadoc tag that can mark a method or class as deprecated while the @link or @see tags can reference the correct replacement in the source code [18]. Pharo[1] has a powerful deprecation engine called *Deprewriter* [13]. It allows library developers to add transformation rules to their method deprecations specifying the replacements. When a deprecated method is invoked, Deprewriter identifies the call-site at run-time and uses the rule to update the client code without interrupting its execution [28, 31, 32].

However, developers of real projects do not always follow good deprecation practices. They tend to introduce breaking changes to the APIs by renaming or removing certain classes, methods, or fields without deprecating them first [5, 40, 41]. Also, several large-scale studies of popular software projects have revealed that the proportion of deprecations that contain a helpful replacement message (in a form of comment, string, annotation, etc.) is only 66.7% for Java, 77.8% for C# [7], and 67% for JavaScript [23].

Multiple approaches have been proposed to support client developers by automatically inferring missing messages. Dig *et al.,* [11] proposed to detect refactorings between the two versions of the library based of the textual similarity of source code and the similarity of references. Schaffer et al. [34], Dagenais *et al.,* [9], and Hora et al. [15] mined frequent method call replacements in the commit history of a library to learn how it adapted to its own changes. Pandita *et al.,* [24] and Alrubaye *et al.,* [1] used a similar technique to help client developers replace dependencies to one library with dependencies to another one. Teyton et al. [38] and Brito *et al.,* [7] recommend replacements by learning from client systems that have already updated their code.

In this work, we look at the problem from the perspective of library developers. We propose an approach and a tool called *DepMiner* to help them identify breaking changes before the release, understand when and by whom they were introduced, and find the potential replacements that could be suggested to the clients. We generate the recommendations in the form of transformation rules that can be used by Pharo's Deprewriter. Inspired by the existing approaches that were proposed to support the client developers [9, 15, 34], our approach is based on the frequent method call analysis. The main differences are: (a) we recommend replacements *before* the release which makes it impossible to rely

---

[1] Pharo is a dynamically-typed object oriented programming language and IDE: https://pharo.org/.

on the clients that were already updated; (b) Pharo is a dynamically-typed language, which means that we can not rely of type information when analyzing method call replacements; (c) Pharo has no explicit method visibility (*i.e.,* public or private specifiers), which makes it hard to define the API. DepMiner can be extended to work with other increasingly popular dynamically-typed languages such as JavaScript, Python, Ruby, etc.

To evaluate our approach, we applied *DepMiner* to 5 diverse open-source projects that were implemented in Pharo and suggested its recommendations to the developers of those projects. 138 recommendations generated by our tool were confirmed by developers. 63 generated deprecations were accepted as pull requests into the projects.

The rest of this paper is structured as follows. In Sect. 2, we briefly describe the Deprewriter tool in Pharo. In Sect. 3, we discuss the problem of supporting library developers and the challenges that arise when dealing with this problem in Pharo. In Sect. 4, we describe our proposed approach and explain the underlying data mining algorithm. In Sect. 5, we evaluate our approach by comparing the generated transformation rules to the ones that are already present in the source code and by performing a developer study. Finally, in Sect. 6, we explain the limitations of our approach.

2   Deprewriter: Transforming Deprecations in Pharo

Pharo allows developers to enrich deprecations with code transformation rules [13]. If a client system invokes the deprecated method, its source code is automatically fixed during execution to call the replacement:

```
1  isSpecial
2    self
3      deprecated: 'Renamed to #needsFullDefinition'
4      transformWith: '`@rec isSpecial'
5                  -> '`@rec needsFullDefinition'.
6    ↑ self needsFullDefinition
```

Lines 2–5 of the code above demonstrate the syntax of transforming deprecations in Pharo: method isSpecial (name in the first line) is deprecated with a message for the user 'Renamed to #needsFullDefinition' and a transformation rule that replaces method calls to isSpectial with calls to needsFullDefinition. The transformation rule consists of two parts: the *antecedent*, matches the method call that should be replaced; the *consequent*, defines the replacement. '@rec and '@arg are rewriting variables matching respectively the receiver of the invocation and its argument.

Transforming deprecations are a powerful technique that can save time for client developers. Because now, instead of reading the source code of a library and looking for the correct replacement, they only need to run the unit tests of their project to have their code fixed automatically.

3 Why Do We Need to Support Library Developers?

To understand the propagation of transforming deprecations, we have extracted all deprecated methods from v8.0.0 of the Pharo Project[2] We discovered that out of 470 valid deprecations in Pharo 8, 190 deprecations (40%) do not contain transformation rules. Out of those 190 non-transforming deprecations, 41 (22%) can have a simple transformation rule that can be generated automatically; 85 deprecations (45%) require developers with project expertise to provide extra information (additional argument, default value, etc.) and write a rule manually; the other 64 deprecations (34%) are complex and can not be expressed using the language for transformation rules that is used in Pharo. This indicates that developers don't always write transformation rules for their deprecations. Similar trends can be observed in other programming languages. For example, according to large-scale studies of software systems, the proportion of deprecations that do not contain a helpful replacement message (in a form of comment, string, annotation, etc.) is 33% for Java, 22% for C# [7], and 33% for JavaScript [23].

Those observations demonstrate the need for an automated tool to recommend the replacement messages for method deprecations. There are two main challenges when implementing such a tool for Pharo:

Challenge 1: Absence of Method Visibility. Languages like Java and C++ have public, private, and protected keywords that can help identify methods that are meant to be used by clients and can be considered as part of API. However, in languages like Python or Pharo all methods are public [35]. Sometimes Python developers use underscores at the beginning of method names to mark them as "private" but it is more of a good practice than a strict requirement and this practice is not always followed. Although Pharo developers often adopt different practices to mark methods as private, none of those practices are universally adopted by the Pharo community.

Challenge 2: Absence of Static Type Information. Pharo is a dynamically-typed programming language [21,37]. The absence of static type information complicates the task of identifying correct method mappings between the old and the new version because it is not easy to map method calls in the source code to the actual method implementations. We also do not know the argument types. This has an important implication that we can get a combinatorial explosion when analysing a sequence of messages. The research community has proposed type inference for dynamically-typed languages [14,25–27,36,37] or use dynamic type information collected by the Virtual Machine to get concrete types [22]. But such type inferencers often do not cover the full language [37] or are not applicable

---

[2] Pharo is a programming language and an IDE written entirely in itself. This can be a source of confusion. In this section, we discuss the analysis of how transforming deprecations, introduced into Pharo (an open-source project with over 150 contributors), were used by its developers to deprecate methods in other parts of the same project. In other words, we study how Pharo developers use the rewriting functionality of Pharo to deprecate methods in Pharo.

to large code bases [36]. In this paper, we do not perform type inference and consider that the type information is missing, which constitutes a challenge for the data mining algorithm.

4   DepMiner: Recommending Transforming Deprecations by Mining the Commit History

We propose to assist library developers in the task of detecting the missed deprecation opportunities and finding proper replacements for the deprecated methods by mining frequent method call replacements from the commit history. Our approach consists of four steps:

1. Identifying the methods that belong to the old API and the new API of the project.
2. Collecting the database of method call replacements from the commit history.
3. Mining frequent method call replacements using the A-Priori algorithm for frequent itemsets mining.
4. Generating deprecations with transformation rules.

Identifying Methods of the Old and the New API. As we have discussed in Sect. 3 (Challenge 1), all methods in Pharo are public in the sense that clients can access them, however not all of those methods are meant to be used. To deal with this challenge, we define several categories of methods in Pharo that can be considered private: (a) *initialize methods*—they act like constructors in Pharo; (b) *unit test methods*, including setUp, tearDown, and methods of mock classes; (c) *example methods*; (d) *baseline methods*—define project structure and dependencies; (e) *help methods*—a form of documentation; (f) *methods in "private" protocols*—any protocol that includes the word "private". We implemented heuristics to infer the visibility of methods in Pharo and released them in a public repository[3]. With that information, we define two sets of methods: API_{old}—"public" methods in the old version, and API_{new}—"public" methods in the new version.

Collecting Method Changes from the Commit History. Given the history of commits between the old version and the new version, we extract method changes from every commit. A *method change* describes how one specific method was changed by a given commit. For each method change, we parse the source code of a method before and after it was changed and extract a set of method calls from each version. As a difference between those two sets, we get the sets of deleted and added method calls for every method change. We remove all deleted method calls that were not part of API_{old} and all added method calls that are not part of API_{new}. Because Pharo is a dynamically-typed language, we do not know which implementation of a method will be executed (see Sect. 3, Challenge 2). As a result, many method calls in our dataset are false positives, because they call the method with the same name as the one in API_{old} and API_{new}, but in

---

[3] https://anonymous.4open.science/r/VisibilityDeductor-EF86.

reality that method is called from a different library (*e.g.*, methods such as add() or asString() can be implemented by different classes). To deal with this problem and reduce the noise in our data, we choose a threshold K and remove all method changes that have more than K added or more than K deleted method calls (by experimenting with different values of K, for this project we selected $K = 3$). We also removed all calls to highly polymorphic methods such as = and printOn:. Finally, we removed all method changes for which either the set of deleted or the set of added calls was empty.

Mining Frequent Method Call Replacements. After collecting the dataset of method changes from the commit history, we apply a data mining algorithm to find all frequent subsets of method call replacements. This technique was inspired by the work of Schäfer *et al.*, [34], Hora *et al.*, [15], and Dagenais *et al.*, [10] who proposed similar history-based approaches to support the clients of Java libraries. In terms of market basket analysis, each method change can be represented as a transaction or an itemset. To do that, we merge the sets of added and deleted calls in a method into a single set. For example, {deleted(isEmpty), deleted(not), deleted(add), added(new), added(isNotEmpty)}. By selecting a minimum support threshold min_{sup}, we use a data mining algorithm such as A-Priori, Eclat, or FP-Growth to find all combinations of method calls that appear in different method changes at least min_{sup} times (frequent itemsets). Then we construct association rules by putting all deleted method calls into the *antecedent* (left hand side) and all added method calls into the *consequent* (right hand side). We remove the rules with empty antecedent or empty consequent. For each association rule $I \rightarrow J$, we calculate its confidence—the probability that a set of deleted calls I appear jointly with added calls J and not with something else:

$$confidence(I \rightarrow J) = \frac{support(I \cup J)}{support(I)}$$

We select a confidence threshold min_{conf} and filter out all association rules that do not reach this threshold. The current implementation of Deprewriter supports only one-to-one (one antecedent, one consequent) and one-to-many rules (one antecedent, several consequents)—the ones that define the replacement of *one* method call (the method from the old API that is being deprecated) with one or more method calls. Therefore, we remove all many-to-one and many-to-many rules from the collection of association rules.

Generating Recommendations. Based on two sets of methods, API_{old} and API_{new}, and the collection of association rules *Assoc*, mined from the method changes, we can now provide recommendations to library developers:

1. **Proposed deprecations**—we find all methods of the old API that were deleted without being deprecated (every method m such that $m \in API_{old}$ and $m \notin API_{new}$). If we can find at least one association rule in *Assoc* that defines the replacement for a given method m, then we recommend

to reintroduce m into the new version of a project with deprecation and a transformation rule if it can be generated.

2. **Transformation rules for existing deprecations**—first we identify all manually deprecated methods from API_{new} that do not contain a transformation rule. For every such method m, if we can find at least one association rule $a \in Assoc$ that defines the replacement for m, we recommend to insert a transformation rule into the deprecation of m either automatically (in case the transformation rule can be inferred from a, as we will discuss below) or semi-automatically (in case we can only show the association rule a to developers and ask them to write a transformation rule manually).

Transformation rules of the form '@rec selector1: '@arg → '@rec selector2: '@arg are generated automatically from the association rule such as {selector1:} → {selector2:} only if:

- association rule is one-to-one (one deleted method call replaced with one added method call),
- deleted and added method calls have the same number of arguments,
- deleted and added method calls are defined in the same class of the new version of the project (and therefore can have the same receiver).

If one of those conditions is not satisfied, the transformation rule can not be generated and must be written manually by a developer. In those cases, we only show to developers the association rule together with the examples of method changes in which those rules appeared and ask them to write a transformation rule manually.

5   Evaluation

We have implemented our approach in a prototype tool for Pharo called *Dep-Miner*.[4] Our implementation is based on the A-Priori algorithm for mining frequent itemsets. We have applied *DepMiner* to several open-source projects and asked core developers of those projects to review the recommendations produced by DepMiner.

5.1   Evaluation Setup

Selected Projects. For this study, we have selected five open-source projects:

- **Pharo**[5]—a large and mature system with more than 150 contributors, containing the language core, the IDE, and various libraries.

---

[4] https://anonymous.4open.science/r/DepMiner-0D5B.
[5] Pharo is an open-source project written in Pharo programming language (see footnote in Sect. 3), https://github.com/pharo-project/pharo.

- **Moose Core**[6]—Moose is a large platform for data and source code analysis. It consists of multiple repositories, we focus only on the core repository of Moose.
- **Famix**[7]—generic library that provides an abstract representation of source code in multiple programming languages. Famix is part of the Moose project.
- **Pillar**[8]—a markup syntax and tool-suite to generate documentation, books, websites and slides.
- **DataFrame**[9]—a specialized collection for data analysis that implements a rich API for querying and transforming datasets.

We selected such projects because: (1) we were able to interview and ask maintainers to validate the proposed deprecations, (2) the projects evolved over several versions and are still under active development, (3) we wanted to compare the performance of *DepMiner* on the projects with different maturity and complexity levels.

For this study, we define three types of projects:

- **Tool**—a project that is designed for the end users (in the experiment: Moose, Pillar). For example, a text editor, a website, or a smartphone app. In many cases, APIs of those projects do not change that much (e.g. poorly named method that is not called by external projects might not be renamed) and when they do change, deprecations are rarely introduced.
- **Library**—a project that is supposed to be used as dependency by other projects (in the experiment: Famix, DataFrame). For example, a data structure, a networking library, or a library for numeric computations. Projects of this type must have a stable API and good versioning. They are most likely to introduce deprecations.
- **SDK**—a special type of project that describes Pharo. It is a combination of multiple different projects. Pharo has many users and even small changes to API can break software that is built with Pharo. This means that deprecations are very important for this type of projects.

Table 1. Selected software projects

Project	Type	Old version	New version	Commits
Pharo	SDK	v8.0.0	af41f85	3,465
Moose Core	Tool	v7.0.0	v8.0.0	1,519
Famix	Library	a5c90ff	v1.0.1	948
Pillar	Tool	v8.0.0	v8.0.12	508
DataFrame	Library	v1.0	v2.0	225

---

[6] https://github.com/moosetechnology/Moose.
[7] https://github.com/moosetechnology/Famix.
[8] https://github.com/pillar-markup/pillar.
[9] https://github.com/PolyMathOrg/DataFrame.

Two Versions of Each Project. To mine the repetitive changes and propose deprecations, we must first select two versions of each project: the *new version* for which we will propose the deprecations and the *old version* to which we compare the new version of the project. All patterns will then be mined from the slice of the commit history between those two versions. Table 1 lists the two versions of each project that we have loaded as well as the number of commits between those two versions.

Mining Frequent Method Call Replacements. We used DepMiner to mine frequent method call replacements from the histories of those projects and recommend deprecations with transformation rules. In Table 2, we report the minimum support and minimum confidence thresholds that were used to initialize the A-Priori algorithm. The minimum support threshold for each project was selected experimentally. We started with a large support threshold = 15 (meaning that we are only interested in replacements that happened at least 15 times) and decreased it until the number of generated recommendation seemed sufficiently large. The confidence threshold was selected based on the number of method changes and the number of rules that *DepMiner* generated for a selected support value. For Pharo and Famix we can expect rules with confidence of at least 0.4. For other projects, we limit confidence to 0.1. In the last two columns of Table 2, we present the number of association rules (frequent method call replacements) that were found by *DepMiner* given the settings discussed above, and the number of rules that can automatically generate the transformation rules of the form '@rec deletedSelector: '@arg → '@rec addedSelector: '@arg (only one-to-one rules where deleted and added selectors have the same number of arguments).

Table 2. Association rules mined from the commit history

Project	Min sup.	Min conf.	Assoc. rules	Transforming
Pharo	5	0.4	377	152
Moose Core	2	0.1	88	40
Famix	4	0.4	149	60
Pillar	2	0.1	49	16
DataFrame	5	0.1	22	7

5.2   Evaluation by Project Developers

We have performed a first developer study of our tool involving the core developers from each project listed in Sect. 5.1. We asked 4 developers with different areas of expertise to validate the recommendations generated for Pharo and one developer for each of the other 4 projects (two developers had expertise in two projects each so in total, our study involved 6 developers).

To each developer, we showed the pretrained *DepMiner* tool with recommended methods to deprecate and recommended transformation rules to insert into the existing deprecations. The developers had to select the changes which, in their opinion, should be merged into the project. *DepMiner* allows its users to browse multiple version of the project as well as the commits history. Each recommendation is supported by the list of commits in which the given method call replacement has appeared. This allowed developers who participated in our study to make an informed decision. For the Pharo project we considered recommendation accepted if it was accepted by at least one developer (because different developers might know different parts of the whole system).

Proposed Deprecations. Table 3 reports the numbers of deprecations that were recommended to developers for each project (column *Recommended*), the number of those recommendations that were accepted (column *Accepted*), and the number of those accepted recommendations that contain an automatically generated transformation rule (column *Transforming*). Each recommended deprecation is a method that was deleted from the project without being deprecated first and which we propose to re-introduce with the recommended replacement.

Table 3. Number of recommended deprecations accepted by developers

Project	Recommended	Accepted	Transforming
Pharo	113	61	56
Moose Core	33	1	1
Famix	87	68	28
Pillar	1	0	0
DataFrame	11	4	4

One can see that *DepMiner* was very effective in generating recommendations for Pharo (113 recommendations, 61 accepted), Famix (87 recommendations, 68 accepted), and DataFrame library (11 recommendations, 4 accepted) but rather ineffective on Moose Core (33 recommendations, 1 accepted) and Pillar (1 recommendation, 0 accepted).

The different performance on those projects can not be explained by their size. For example, the DataFrame project is the smallest one in our list, but out of 11 deprecations generated by *DepMiner*, 4 deprecations were accepted. On the other hand, for the Pillar project, which is 10 times larger in terms of the number of methods, only 1 deprecation was generated and it was not accepted. Further study is required to explain the differences between DataFrame and Pillar, but we can speculate that bad performance on Pillar is caused by the low variability of API. Methods of DataFrame were often renamed, removed, or reorganised, which was reflected in test cases and picked up by *DepMiner*. On the other hand, the API of Pillar remained stable even though new functionality was added to it and many bugs were fixed.

Missing Rules. The other type of recommendations that we showed to developers were transformation rules for existing non-transforming deprecations. Table 4 reports the number of existing deprecations that are missing a transformation rule, the number of recommendations that DepMiner managed to generate for those deprecations, and finally the number of recommendations that were accepted by developers.

Table 4. Number of missing rules accepted by developers

Project	Missing	Recommended	Accepted
Pharo	189	6	2
Moose Core	2	0	0
Famix	27	2	2
Pillar	0	0	0
DataFrame	0	0	0

Deprecations that are missing the transformation rule (the non-transforming deprecations) represent either complicated cases for which the transformation rule can not be provided (e.g. method was deleted without replacement) or simple cases for which developers forgot to write a rule. As we mentioned in Sect. 3, for 22% of non-transforming deprecations the transformation rule could be generated automatically (assuming that we know the correct replacement), the other 78% of non-transforming deprecations require a complex rule that must be written manually. *DepMiner* proposed 6 transformation rules for existing non-transforming deprecations in Pharo (2 of which were accepted) as well as 2 transformation rules for Famix (both were accepted).

Pull Requests. Out of 5 projects that we used in our study, only Pharo Project was preparing an upcoming release. We applied DepMiner to the latest commit of the development version of Pharo and this allowed us to submit the recommendations that were confirmed by developers as pull requests. All 61 confirmed deprecations and 2 confirmed transformation rules for existing deprecations were merged into the v9.0.0 release of Pharo.

6   Limitations of Our Approach

Unused/Untested Methods. Our approach is based on library's usage of its own API. This means that we can not infer anything for methods that are not used by the library itself but only intended for clients. Test cases play the role of clients of the library's API, so for the methods that are well tested, we can have enough input to identify the correct replacement for them. But if a method is not used by the library and not covered by test, then its deletion or renaming will not be reflected anywhere else in the source code.

Reflective Operations. Modern programming languages offer reflective operations [8,29]. They allow developers to invoke methods programmatically and create generic and powerful tools. However, since some methods can be invoked reflectively for example passing the name of the method to be invoked in a variable, when a different argument is passed to a reflective call, our tool cannot identify such change. Most static analysers ignore such case [4].

Unordered Set of Method Calls. Our tool is based on mining method call replacement by comparing the set of calls that were deleted from the source code of a modified method to the set of calls that were added to it. We do not take into account the order of method calls, the distance between them or how they are composed: a().b() or a(b()). This is a limitation of our approach because: (1) sometimes deleted and added method calls are located far away in source code and not related to each other; (2) if one method call is being replaced with two or more method calls, we do not know how they should be composed.

7   Related Work

Breaking Changes. Breaking changes are the code modifications in all API elements that break backward compatibility [12]. In their large-scale analysis of Java libraries, Xavier *et al.,* [40] discovered that 28% of API changes break backward compatibility however, on the median, only 2.54% of clients are impacted by them. In their follow-up study, Xavier *et al.,* [41] performed a survey of developers to understand why they introduce breaking changes into their projects. They identified five reasons: library simplification, refactoring, bug fixes, dependency changes, project policy. This study was later extended by Brito *et al.,* [5] who reported that 47% of breaking changes are due to refactorings. These results can be complemented by the previous study by Dig and Johnson [12] who analysed breaking changes in five Java systems and discovered that 81–100% of them are caused by refactorings. Those findings are important for our study because changes that are introduced by refactorings (e.g. renaming, replacement, spitting, etc.) ofter require simple repetitive fixes in the client code that can be expressed with transformation rules.

Impact of Deprecations. Robbes *et al.,* [30] studied the impact of API changes, and in particular deprecations, on Pharo and Squeak ecosystems. They report that the majority of client systems are updated over a day, but in some cases the update takes longer and is performed only partially. Sawant *et al.,* [33] report similar results for Java. Hora *et al.,* [16,17] complemented the previous studies by analysing the impact of API evolution on Pharo ecosystem, but focusing only on those changes which are not related to deprecations. They claim that API changes have large impact on the ecosystem and most of the changes that they found can be implemented as rules in static analysis tools. Several authors have also explored the effectiveness of deprecation messages. Large-scale empirical studies of software written in Java and C# [6,7] as well as JavaScript [23] revealed that 22–33% of deprecations in those languages are not supported by replacement messages. In their study of Pharo ecosystem, Robbes *et al.*, [30] also showed that almost 50% of deprecation messages do not help to identify the correct replacement.

Library Migration and Update. Mining the commit history to find a mapping between two versions of API is not a new idea. Similar problems were targeted in the context of library update (updating client system to depend on a new version of the external library) and library migration (replacing the dependency on one library with that on a different library). First approaches in this area were based on static code analysis and the textual similarity of method signatures [19,43]. Wu *et al.*, [39] proposed an approach that combined call dependency and text similarity analyses. Schäfer *et al.*, [34] proposed to mine library update rules from already updated client systems. The following studies analysed the commit history between the two versions of a library [10,20] and proposed changes that should be applied to client systems. Teyton *et al.*, [38] used data mining and propose rules for library migration by learning from the commit histories of already migrated clients. Hora *et al.*, [15] proposed a similar approach to find method mappings between different releases of the same library. Pandita *et al.*, [24] approached the problem of library migration by analysing textual similarity of documentation from different libraries. Alrubaye *et al.*, [2] proposed a novel machine learning approach that inferred the mapping between the API elements of two different library by extracting various features from library documentation and solving a classification problem. Our approach of mining the commit history was inspired by previous works in the domain of library migration and update. However, instead of proposing migration rules to client developers, we propose transforming deprecations to library developers.

Recommending Deprecations and Replacements. To the best of our knowledge, our study is the first to propose supporting library developers by recommending deprecations and generating replacement rules. Brito *et al.*, [7] recommend replacement messages for deprecations by learning from client systems that have already identified the correct replacements and updated their code. Our approach takes information from the history of a library and therefore does not depend on migrated clients (which might not be available or may not cover the full API). Xi *et al.*, [42] designed an automatic process for migrating deprecating API to its replacement in client systems. However, their approach is based on the replacement messages in code documentation. One of the goals of our approach is to generate those replacement messages when they are not known.

8   Conclusion

Method deprecation is a powerful technique for supporting the evolution of software libraries and informing client developers about the upcoming breaking changes to the API. We proposed to mine the frequent method call replacements from the commit history of a library and use them to recommend method deprecations and transformation rules. We implemented our approach for Pharo IDE in a tool called *DepMiner*. We applied our tool to five open-source projects and asked 6 core developers from those projects to accept or reject the recommended changes. In total, 134 proposed deprecations were accepted by developers as well as 4 transformation rules for the existing deprecations. 61 new deprecations and 2 transformations rules for existing deprecations were integrated into the Pharo project.

Acknowledgments. We want to thank all developers who participated in our experiment and helped us evaluate the recommendations, particularly Guillermo Polito, Pablo Tesone, Marcus Denker, and Benoît Verhaeghe. We are also grateful to the Arolla software company for financing this research.

References

1. Alrubaye, H., Mkaouer, M.W., Ouni, A.: On the use of information retrieval to automate the detection of third-party java library migration at the method level. In: ICPC 2019 (2019)
2. Alrubaye, H., Mkaouer, M.W., Khokhlov, I., Reznik, L., Ouni, A., Mcgoff, J.: Learning to recommend third-party library migration opportunities at the API level. Appl. Soft Comput., 106–140 (2020)
3. Baldassarre, M.T., Bianchi, A., Caivano, D., Visaggio, G.: An industrial case study on reuse oriented development. In: 21st IEEE International Conference on Software Maintenance (ICSM 2005), pp. 283–292. IEEE (2005)
4. Bodden, E., Sewe, A., Sinschek, J., Oueslati, H., Mezini, M.: Taming reflection: aiding static analysis in the presence of reflection and custom class loaders. In: Proceedings of the 33rd International Conference on Software Engineering, ICSE 2011, pp. 241–250. ACM, New York (2011)
5. Brito, A., Valente, M.T., Xavier, L., Hora, A.: You broke my code: understanding the motivations for breaking changes in APIs. Empir. Softw. Eng. **25**(2), 1458–1492 (2020)
6. Brito, G., Hora, A., Valente, M.T., Robbes, R.: Do developers deprecate APIs with replacement messages? A large-scale analysis on Java systems. In: 2016 IEEE 23rd International Conference on Software Analysis, Evolution, and Reengineering (SANER), vol. 1, pp. 360–369. IEEE (2016)
7. Brito, G., Hora, A., Valente, M.T., Robbes, R.: On the use of replacement messages in API deprecation: an empirical study. J. Syst. Softw. **137**, 306–321 (2018)
8. Callau, O., Robbes, R., Rothlisberger, D., Tanter, E.: How developers use the dynamic features of programming languages: the case of smalltalk. In: Mining Software Repositories International Conference (MSR 2011) (2011)
9. Dagenais, B., Robillard, M.P.: Recommending adaptive changes for framework evolution. In: Proceedings of the 30th International Conference on Software Engineering, ICSE 2008, pp. 481–490. ACM, New York (2008)
10. Dagenais, B., Robillard, M.P.: Recommending adaptive changes for framework evolution. ACM Trans. Softw. Eng. Methodol. (TOSEM) **20**(4), 1–35 (2011)

11. Dig, D., Comertoglu, C., Marinov, D., Johnson, R.: Automated detection of refactorings in evolving components. In: Thomas, D. (ed.) ECOOP 2006. LNCS, vol. 4067, pp. 404–428. Springer, Heidelberg (2006). https://doi.org/10.1007/11785477_24
12. Dig, D., Johnson, R.: How do APIs evolve? A story of refactoring. J. Softw. Maintenance Evol. Res. Pract. (JSME) **18**(2), 83–107 (2006)
13. Ducasse, S., Polito, G., Zaitsev, O., Denker, M., Tesone, P.: Deprewriter: On the fly rewriting method deprecations. JOT **21**, 1–23 (2022)
14. Furr, M., hoon (David) An, J., Foster, J.S., Hicks, M.: Static type inference for Ruby. In: Symposium on Applied Computing (SAC 2009) (2009)
15. Hora, A., Etien, A., Anquetil, N., Ducasse, S., Valente, M.T.: APIEvolutionMiner: keeping API evolution under control. In: Proceedings of the Software Evolution Week (CSMR-WCRE 2014) (2014)
16. Hora, A., Robbes, R., Anquetil, N., Etien, A., Ducasse, S., Valente, M.T.: How do developers react to API evolution? The Pharo ecosystem case. In: Proceedings of the 31st IEEE International Conference on Software Maintenance, pp. 251–260 (2015)
17. Hora, A., Robbes, R., Tulio Valente, M., Anquetil, N., Etien, A., Ducasse, S.: How do developers react to API evolution? A large-scale empirical study. Software Qual. J. **26**, 161–191 (2018)
18. Oracle: how and when to deprecate APIs. Java se documentation. https://docs.oracle.com/javase/7/docs/technotes/guides/javadoc/deprecation/deprecation.html. Accessed 19 Apr 2021
19. Kim, M., Notkin, D., Grossman, D.: Automatic inference of structural changes for matching across program versions. In: 29th International Conference on Software Engineering (ICSE 2007), pp. 333–343. IEEE (2007)
20. Meng, S., Wang, X., Zhang, L., Mei, H.: A history-based matching approach to identification of framework evolution. In: 2012 34th International Conference on Software Engineering (ICSE), pp. 353–363. IEEE (2012)
21. Milner, R.: A theory of type polymorphism in programming. J. Comput. Syst. Sci. **17**, 348–375 (1978)
22. Milojković, N., Béra, C., Ghafari, M., Nierstrasz, O.: Inferring types by mining class usage frequency from inline caches. In: International Workshop on Smalltalk Technologies IWST 2016, Prague, Czech Republic, August 2016
23. Nascimento, R., Brito, A., Hora, A., Figueiredo, E.: Javascript API deprecation in the wild: a first assessment. In: 2020 IEEE 27th International Conference on Software Analysis, Evolution and Reengineering (SANER), pp. 567–571. IEEE (2020)
24. Pandita, R., Jetley, R.P., Sudarsan, S.D., Williams, L.: Discovering likely mappings between APIs using text mining. In: 2015 IEEE 15th International Working Conference on Source Code Analysis and Manipulation (SCAM), pp. 231–240. IEEE (2015)
25. Passerini, N., Tesone, P., Ducasse, S.: An extensible constraint-based type inference algorithm for object-oriented dynamic languages supporting blocks and generic types. In: International Workshop on Smalltalk Technologies (IWST 14), August 2014
26. Pluquet, F., Marot, A., Wuyts, R.: Fast type reconstruction for dynamically typed programming languages. In: Proceedings of the 5th Symposium on Dynamic Languages, DLS 2009, pp. 69–78. ACM, New York (2009)

27. Ren, B.M., Foster, J.S.: Just-in-time static type checking for dynamic languages. In: Conference on Programming Language Design and Implementation (PLDI) (2016)
28. Renggli, L., Gîrba, T., Nierstrasz, O.: Embedding languages without breaking tools. In: D'Hondt, T. (ed.) ECOOP 2010. LNCS, vol. 6183, pp. 380–404. Springer, Heidelberg (2010). https://doi.org/10.1007/978-3-642-14107-2_19
29. Richards, G., Hammer, C., Burg, B., Vitek, J.: The eval that men do: a large-scale study of the use of eval in Javascript applications. In: Proceedings of Ecoop 2011 (2011)
30. Robbes, R., Röthlisberger, D., Tanter, É.: Extensions during software evolution: do objects meet their promise? In: Noble, J. (ed.) ECOOP 2012. LNCS, vol. 7313, pp. 28–52. Springer, Heidelberg (2012). https://doi.org/10.1007/978-3-642-31057-7_3
31. Roberts, D., Brant, J., Johnson, R.E.: A refactoring tool for Smalltalk. Theor. Pract. Object Syst. (TAPOS) **3**(4), 253–263 (1997)
32. Roberts, D., Brant, J., Johnson, R.E., Opdyke, B.: An automated refactoring tool. In: Proceedings of ICAST 1996, Chicago, IL, April 1996
33. Sawant, A.A., Robbes, R., Bacchelli, A.: On the reaction to deprecation of 25,357 clients of 4 + 1 popular Java APIs. In: 2016 IEEE International Conference on Software Maintenance and Evolution (ICSME), pp. 400–410. IEEE (2016)
34. Schäfer, T., Jonas, J., Mezini, M.: Mining framework usage changes from instantiation code. In: Proceedings of the 30th International Conference on Software Engineering, ICSE 2008, pp. 471–480. ACM, New York (2008)
35. Schärli, N., Black, A.P., Ducasse, S.: Object-oriented encapsulation for dynamically typed languages. In: Proceedings of 18th International Conference on Object-Oriented Programming Systems, Languages and Applications (OOPSLA 2004), pp. 130–149, October 2004
36. Spoon, S.A., Shivers, O.: Demand-driven type inference with subgoal pruning: Trading precision for scalability. In: Proceedings of ECOOP 2004, pp. 51–74 (2004)
37. Suzuki, N.: Inferring types in smalltalk. In: Proceedings of the 8th ACM SIGPLAN-SIGACT Symposium on Principles of Programming Languages, pp. 187–199, POPL 1981. ACM Press, New York (1981)
38. Teyton, C., Falleri, J.R., Blanc, X.: Automatic discovery of function mappings between similar libraries. In: 2013 20th Working Conference on Reverse Engineering (WCRE), pp. 192–201. IEEE (2013)
39. Wu, W., Guéhéneuc, Y.G., Antoniol, G., Kim, M.: Aura: a hybrid approach to identify framework evolution. In: 2010 ACM/IEEE 32nd International Conference on Software Engineering, vol. 1, pp. 325–334. IEEE (2010)
40. Xavier, L., Brito, A., Hora, A., Valente, M.T.: Historical and impact analysis of API breaking changes: a large-scale study. In: 2017 IEEE 24th International Conference on Software Analysis, Evolution and Reengineering (SANER), pp. 138–147. IEEE (2017)
41. Xavier, L., Hora, A., Valente, M.T.: Why do we break APIs? First answers from developers. In: 2017 IEEE 24th International Conference on Software Analysis, Evolution and Reengineering (SANER), pp. 392–396. IEEE (2017)
42. Xi, Y., Shen, L., Gui, Y., Zhao, W.: Migrating deprecated API to documented replacement: patterns and tool. In: Proceedings of the 11th Asia-Pacific Symposium on Internetware, pp. 1–10 (2019)
43. Xing, A., Stroulia, E.: API-evolution support with diff-catchup. IEEE Trans. Software Eng. **33**, 818–836 (2007)

Learning and Reuse

Scratching the Surface of `./configure`: Learning the Effects of Compile-Time Options on Binary Size and Gadgets

Xhevahire Tërnava[1]([⊠]), Mathieu Acher[1,2], Luc Lesoil[1], Arnaud Blouin[1,3], and Jean-Marc Jézéquel[1]

[1] Univ Rennes, CNRS, Inria, IRISA - UMR 6074, 35000 Rennes, France
{xhevahire.ternava,mathieu.acher,luc.lesoil,arnaud.blouin,
jean-marc.jezequel}@irisa.fr
[2] Institut Universitaire de France (IUF), Paris, France
[3] INSA Rennes, Rennes, France

Abstract. Numerous software systems are configurable through compile-time options and the widely used `./configure`. However, the combined effects of these options on binary's non-functional properties (size and attack surface) are often not documented, and or not well understood, even by experts. Our goal is to provide automated support for exploring and comprehending the configuration space (*a.k.a.*, surface) of compile-time options using statistical learning techniques. In this paper, we perform an empirical study on four C-based configurable systems. We measure the variation of binary size and attack surface (by quantifying the number of code reuse gadgets) in over 400 compile-time configurations of a subject system. We then apply statistical learning techniques on top of our build infrastructure to identify how compile-time options relate to non-functional properties. Our results show that, by changing the default configuration, the system's binary size and gadgets vary greatly (roughly -79% to 244% and -77% to 30%, respectively). Then, we found out that identifying the most influential options can be accurately learned with a small training set, while their relative importance varies across size and attack surface for the same system. Practitioners can use our approach and artifacts to explore the effects of compile-time options in order to take informed decisions when configuring a system with `./configure`.

Keywords: Configurable systems · Compile-time variability · Binary size · Gadgets · System security · Non-functional properties · Statistical learning

1 Introduction

Modern software systems are highly configurable and expose to the users their abundant configuration options. By enabling or disabling configuration options,

© Springer Nature Switzerland AG 2022
G. Perrouin et al. (Eds.): ICSR 2022, LNCS 13297, pp. 41–58, 2022.
https://doi.org/10.1007/978-3-031-08129-3_3

a software system can be customized for different contexts, such as for different users or hardware with a limited memory size, without the need to modify its source code. But this high flexibility of software systems comes with a cost. A large number of configuration options indeed makes the system complex and threatens its maintenance. First, because *"a significant percentage (up to 54.1%) of parameters are rarely set by any user."* [28] and thus they unnecessarily bloat the software [14]. Then, the disabled options may have security issues or bugs, which might be exploited and threaten the whole system. Further, there is evidence that many software failures arise from misconfiguration [19,29], while finding the cause of a failure among the large set of options is difficult. To reduce the complexity and improve the software configuration quality, there are several approaches [3,15,21,28]. But the large number of configuration options and their enabling/disabling are likely to have an impact also on the non-functional properties of a given system, such as in its binary size and attack surface.

Actually, most of embedded systems, mobile devices, or any resource-constrained devices may exhibit requirements regarding the executable binary size of a software application [11]. Further, from a security perspective, a large code base of any configurable software system increases the possibilities of *gadgets*, that is, of small code chunks that an attacker can chain in order to build an exploit [3,4,21]. Therefore, motivated by concrete requirements in real software systems (*cf.* Sect. 2), it is of great importance to explore the effects of configuration options on these two non-functional properties of a given system. There are approaches on measuring a set of non-functional properties, including the binary size, for a derived software system in the context of software product lines [25,26]. But, there is hardly any work on exploring the compile-time configuration space during a system's build with ./configure, which is extensive on C-based software systems. In particular, we are unaware of works that attempt to measure *(i)* how much vary the executable binary size and gadgets of a system based on its compile-time configuration options, *(ii)* whether some options are more influential than the others, and *(iii)* whether there is a relationship between these two non-functional properties changes. By making explicit these effects, a user may easily find the unneeded and most vulnerable options in order to reach a desired executable binary size, to prevent any code reuse attack, to improve the installation speed, or the occupied memory size of a system on a device.

The contributions of this paper are as follows:

- We provide empirical evidence for the great variation of binary size and attack surface in C-based systems, depending on their applied compile-time configurations. We argue that changing the system's default configuration can be beneficial for its users, but how it should be changed is not trivial.
- Therefore, we made a comparison of different learning techniques to predict binary size and gadget of any compile-time configuration. We then report and qualitatively analyse the influential options and their interactions based on interpretable information of performance prediction models.

– Furthermore, we provide the dataset of our measurements, as well as our scripts, which can be used to reproduce our study.

To accomplish them, we provide the motivation (Sect. 2) and research ques tions to be addressed (Sect. 3). Then, we set up an experiment to answer those questions by studying four popular C-based open-source systems (Sect. 4). Next, we report on the variation of binary size and number of gadgets, measured on a large set of configurations (Sect. 5.1 and 5.2). In addition, we provide an app-roach to find the most influential options on these two non-functional properties and report on them for four systems (Sect. 5.3). We also discuss the costs, bene-fits, and future work (Sect. 6), including threats to validity (Sect. 7) and related work (Sect. 8). Section 9 concludes our paper.

2 Background and Motivation

In this section, we provide a background on the `./configure` flavour for con-figuring C-based systems and on the *number of gadgets*, as an attack surface metric. At the same time, the motivation of our study is presented.

`./configure`. Most of the C-based software systems, which are also the sub-jects of this work, use the GNU autotools (*e.g.*, Autoconf [5]) to help devel-opers to pack and distribute their software to multiple platforms and to facil-itate their configuration and installation by the end-users. All that end-users see is the packed software with the generated *configure* script and *Makefile.in* file. Then, all that is left for the users to do is simply to type the command sequence `./configure && make && make install` in order to configure, build, and install the given software. As most of the C-based systems are configurable through compile-time and run-time options, users can use the `./configure` flavour to customize the targeted software at compile-time. For example, x264 is a video encoder[1] with 39 compile-time options. In case the support for mp4 video encoding is not required, then it is possible to deactivate it by using the `--disable-lsmash` option during the system build, as in the following listing.

```
$ ./configure --disable-lsmash    # It generates Makefile from Makefile.in
$ make                            # It uses Makefile to build the x264
$ make install                    # It uses Makefile to install the x264
```

In this way, the `./configure` makes it possible to customize a software sys-tem with only the needed functionalities. Despite this possibility, a software sys-tem is often installed with off-the-shelf default configuration options. But, there is evidence that system administrators frequently make poor configuration choices, for example, the default settings for Hadoop result in the worst possible perfor-mance [9]. Hence, system administrators often suggest users to customize soft-ware systems to get their desired systems' performance or non-functional proper-ties. Specifically, excluding certain unused functionalities at compile-time is often seen as an opportunity to reduce the system's binary size for cases where it is an

---

[1] x264 settings: http://www.chaneru.com/Roku/HLS/X264_Settings.htm.

important factor, such as in embedded applications. Such an example is `SQLite`, stating that *"If optional features are omitted, the size of the* `SQLite` *library can be reduced below 180KiB."* [2] for which reason `SQLite` is also a popular database engine in memory-constrained devices. But, unlike system administrators, end-users lack the expertise to tune the system to get the right binary size. Basically, they lack knowledge on: Which are the optional compile-time options in a system that should be removed to get a desired binary size? What is the effect of each enabled or disabled option on the system's binary size?

Gadgets. Nowadays, the security of modern software systems is mostly threatened internally, that is, by reusing their existing code, without the need for code injection [21]. This kind of attack allows an attacker to execute arbitrary code on a victim's machine. In this attack, the attacker is able to chain some small code sequences (called *gadgets*) and threaten the security of the system. Basically, the exploited code sequences by the attacker end in a return (RET or JMP) instruction. Therefore, one of the commonly used metrics for measuring the attack surface in a system is *the number of code reuse gadgets* that are available and which can be exploited by an attacker [3,4,21]. Hence, to a certain degree, the attack surface of systems is related to their binary size. Therefore, considering that the security in software systems is important, such as in `SQLite`[3], as few gadgets (smaller binary size) are often desirable to reduce the attack surface in the system. But, end-users lack the knowledge regarding how much the unused compile-time options in their installed system with a default configuration threaten their system? Or, what is the effect of each compile-time option on the system's attack surface?

Though numerous works have considered the performance of software product lines [25,26], little is known about the effects of compile-time options on the system's non-functional properties, namely, on binary size, number of gadgets, and how configuration knowledge related to binary size or attack surface can be effectively recovered. The need to make users aware of the importance of customizing software during `./configure` and system administrators to document the effects of options on binary size and gadgets motivates our work.

3   Research Questions

Motivated by such examples, the goal of this study is to quantify and learn the effects of compile-time options on binary size and attack surface of C-based configurable software systems and which options are of great importance for end-users. To attain this goal, we define the three following research questions.

RQ_1: **What is the effect of compile-time options of a system on its binary size?** To this end, we use four C-based configurable software systems, as subjects, and enable or disable their compile-time options based on two

---

[2] `SQLite`: http://barbra-coco.dyndns.org/sqlite/about.html.
[3] Security in `SQLite`: https://cve.mitre.org/cgi-bin/cvekey.cgi?keyword=sqlite.

Table 1. Four subject systems with their baseline binary size [bytes] and gadgets

Subject		Analysed			Baseline	
System	Description	Commit	#LoC	#Options	Binary size	Gadgets
x264	*Video encoder*	db0d417	114,475	25/39	3,096,112	106,878
nginx	*Web server*	cc73d76	172,368	91/127	4,507,168	29,925
SQLite	*SQL database engine*	385b982	318,496	31/72	8,561,208	67,734
xz	*Data compressor*	e7da44d	37,489	36/88	1,254,536	9,121

scenarios (*cf.* Sect. 4.3). We then record the binary size of each obtained system's executable and compare them with the baseline binary size.

RQ_2: **What is the effect of compile-time options of a system on its attack surface (*a.k.a.,* gadgets)?** To measure the attack surface of a system, we rely on the number of found gadgets in its executable. In addition, we explore whether there is a correlation between the binary size and the number of gadgets for different enabled/disabled compile-time options.

RQ_3: **Which compile-time options are the most influential on the binary size and the gadgets of a software system?** To this end, we use statistical prediction models to predict the influence of compile-time options on the binary size and number of gadgets in our subject systems. We report on interactions among options and discuss qualitatively these options.

4   Experimental Protocol

In this section, we introduce the used subject systems and the experiment settings in order to answer the three research questions.

4.1   Subject Systems

To select a subject system for our study, we used several sources, such as the studied systems by research papers on software variability and software debloating[4], the website openbenchmarking[5], and our knowledge on popular open-source projects. Then, we had into consideration the fact that subjects should contain compile-time configuration options, are open-source, cover different application domains, and are popular projects. To reason on a project's popularity, we used as a proxy the number of stars, commits, and contributors in its git repository.

As the C-based software systems are typical systems that are rich with compile-time configuration options to be handled, we selected four of them as subjects, namely, x264, nginx, SQLite, and xz. Regarding their popularity, all of them have between 86–15.6k stars, 1.3k–23.7k commits, and 17–94 contributors[6].

---

[4] https://www.cesarsotovalero.net/software-debloating-papers#2020.
[5] https://openbenchmarking.org/.
[6] Based on our last check on February 2022.

In Table 1 are given a brief description of each subject system, its respective analysed commit ID in its git repository, size in number of Lines of Code (LoC)[7], and the considered number (versus the overall number) of compile-time options.

4.2 Baseline Configuration

Usually, by using the `./configure --help` option during the build of a C-based system, the available compile-time options are shown as a plain list, including the external libraries and their default values. These are the used options to customize the given system for a specific environment and user context. It is important to note that, each system comes with a default build configuration, that is, each of its compile-time options is by default either enabled or disabled. We refer to this default configuration of a system as its *baseline configuration*.

The baseline configuration of our subject systems is the current configuration in their respective git repository (*cf.* Table 1). In order to exercise with as many compile-time options as possible, we had to install in our environment the external libraries required by each subject. Furthermore, Table 1 presents the executable binary size in bytes and the number of found gadgets[8] for the baseline configuration of each subject system. In the following, we will refer to them as the *baseline binary size* and *baseline number of gadgets*.

4.3 The Conducted Experiment

With all four subject systems, we conducted an experiment in the same environment. Specifically, we first fetched the targeted system from its git repository and compiled it on its default configuration. To make sure that the compilation was successful, we used the compiled system in an elementary example. For instance, we encoded a video using x264, used a run-time option of **nginx**, opened a database using **SQLite**, and compressed a file using **xz**. To later automate the generation of configurations, we manually explored the configuration space of each system, identified the dependencies of its compile-time options, and build its feature model (FM)[9] (their availability is given below).

Next, to answer the research questions RQ_1 and RQ_2, we automatically customized the four subject systems by following these two scenarios.

S_1 : First, each system is customized by **a single compile-time option** at a time. The left value in column #Options in Table 1 shows the number of considered options in each system. It has to be stressed that these options had Boolean or enumerate values. Hence, using them, we built 31 configurations with a single option for x264, 91 for **nginx**, 31 for **SQLite**, and 65 for **xz**.

S_2 : Then, each system is customized by **a mixed set of compile-time options**. In total, we used a significant sample of 400 configurations in each subject

---

[7] Measured using the `cloc` tool: https://github.com/AlDanial/cloc.
[8] Measured using the ROPgadget: https://github.com/JonathanSalwan/ROPgadget.
[9] For this purpose, we used FeatureIDE framework: https://featureide.github.io/.

system. All of these configurations are generated using the random product generator in the FeatureIDE framework.

Finally, to answer RQ_3, we designed the following protocol to identify *influential compile-time* options *i.e.*, options having a statistically significant influence on non-functional properties. There exist several techniques to identify influential options, most of them based on supervised machine learning models[10] predicting the performance properties of our systems. We first rely on the measurement of *feature permutation importance* [16] (in short: feature importance). Feature importance is computed through the observation of the effect on machine learning model accuracy of randomly shuffling each predictor variable. We compute feature importance over random forest [16], the machine learning method leading to the best accuracy in our case[11]. Feature importance gives a score between 0 (no influence) and 1. It is comparable across different problems, *e.g.*, we can compare the influence of the same compile-time option over binary size and gadgets. The measure automatically takes into account all interactions with other features. This is a good property but also a disadvantage since feature interactions are not made explicit. To further understand and mitigate this lack, we consider: *(i)* the coefficients of Lasso [8] with feature interactions for gadgets; and *(ii)* the rules of the decision trees that give information on how features interact. We then confront identified options with the documentation of the project in order to understand whether their effect on size and gadgets make sense from a domain or technical point of view.

Moreover, all steps of our experiment are automated by Python scripts. The used artifacts, such as the Feature Model and over 400 selected configurations of each system, the details to reproduce our experiment, and all the obtained results

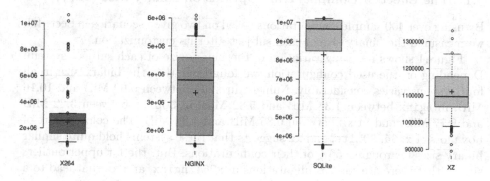

Fig. 1. The variation of binary size in four subject systems

---

[10] Owing to space issue, we place the technical details about our machine learning models in the companion repository and encourage our readers to consult them; the implementation, the chosen learning methods, the choice of metric and the obtained results when predicting the binary size and the number of gadgets of our systems.

[11] See the detailed results at https://github.com/diverse-project/confsurface/blob/main/learning/results.md.

are made available in the git repository https://github.com/diverse-project/confsurface and in zenodo https://doi.org/10.5281/zenodo.6401250.

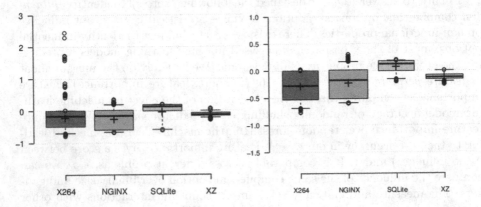

Fig. 2. Binary size baseline comparisons

Fig. 3. Gadgets baseline comparisons

5 Results

We now report the results and observations with regard to our research questions.

5.1 The Effect of Compile-Time Options on Binary Size (RQ_1)

By using over 400 sample configurations based on two given scenarios in Sect. 4.3, we measured the binary size of each subject after its customization.

Figure 1 shows resulting variation of the binary size of each subject system. Depending on the used configuration, we found out that the binary size in all four systems varies considerably. Namely, in x264 between 0.62 MiB and 10.16 MiB, in nginx between 1.38 MiB and 5.82 MiB, in SQLite between 3.22 MiB and 9.77 MiB, and in xz between 0.85 MiB and 1.28 MiB. The colored part of box plots of x264, SQLite, and xz suggests that these systems hold quite similar binary sizes for roughly 50% of their configurations. But, the far upper outliers signify that there are some configurations in x264, nginx, and xz that lead to a far higher binary size. Still, the bottom outliers suggest that x264, SQLite, and xz can reach a far smaller binary size in a considerable number of configurations. Figure 2 shows the relative difference, in percentage, of a system's binary size after its customization to the baseline binary size. By comparing with the *baseline binary size* given in Table 1, it can be observed that most of the configurations in three of the four systems lead to a smaller binary size than their baseline binary size (0 percentage in Fig. 2 is the baseline value). Specifically, 56% of configurations in x264, 68% in nginx, 28% in SQLite, and 92% in xz provide a smaller binary size. Fewer configurations increase the system's binary size, namely, 6% in x264, 32% in nginx, 67% in SQLite, and 1% in xz. Then, 38%, 5%, and 7% of the configurations in x264, SQLite, and xz, respectively, have the same binary size as in their default configuration. Only in nginx, for any other configuration that is different from its baseline configuration, its binary size is always different.

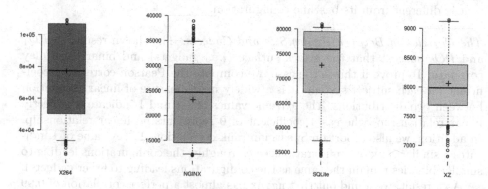

Fig. 4. The variation of gadgets in four subject systems

Answer to RQ_1 : These results show that compile-time options of a system have a noticeable effect on its executable binary size. Based on four popular systems, changing the system's default configuration, it is very likely (in 61% of the cases) that the system's binary size will be reduced, but it is less likely (in 26% of the cases) that it will be increased or remained the same (in 13% of the cases). Then, the binary size on average decreases for more bytes (36%) than that it increases (33%). Hence, the compile-time customization of a software has mainly a positive effect on its binary size.

5.2   The Effect of Compile-Time Options on Attack Surface (RQ_2)

Using the same sample of configurations, S_1 and S_2 in Sect. 4.3, we measured the number of code reuse gadgets of each system after its customization.

The Variation of the Number of Gadgets. Figure 4 shows resulting variation of the number of gadgets in each subject system. By changing the baseline configuration of a system, we found out that the number of gadgets in all four systems varies considerably. Specifically, in x264 between 25K and 109K, in nginx between 12K and 39K, in SQLite between 54K and 81K, and in xz between 7K and 9K gadgets. The tall box plots of four systems suggest that each system configuration provides a customized system with a quite different number of gadgets. Figure 3 shows the relative difference, in percentage, of a system's gadgets after its customization to the baseline gadgets. By comparing with the *baseline number of gadgets* given in Table 1, it can be noticed that most of the configurations in x264, nginx, and xz (61%, 68%, and 92%, respectively) lead to a smaller number of gadgets than the baseline configuration (0% in Fig. 3 is the baseline value). Whereas, only 30% of them are in SQLite. Still, only in a few configurations the number of gadgets is increased (1% in x264, 32% in nginx, and 0.43% in xz) or remained the same (38% in x264, 4% in SQLite, and 7% in xz) with the baseline number of gadgets. As with its binary size (*cf.* Sect. 5.1), the number of gadgets in nginx is always different for any other configuration that is different from its baseline configuration.

The Correlation Between Binary Size and Gadgets. The shown results in RQ_1 and RQ_2 suggest that the attack surface (*i.e.,* gadgets) and binary size may correlate. To prove if this is the case, we compute the Pearson correlation coefficient for each subject system. It is a widely used measure of linear correlation between two distributions. The extreme values of -1 and 1 indicate a perfectly linear relationship, whereas a coefficient of 0 represents no linear relationship. In addition, we also report on Spearman rank correlation [12]. A value of 1 indicates a similar rank of configurations (*e.g.,* roughly, the configurations leading to smaller binaries remain the same as the configurations leading to fewer gadgets).

As a result, we found out that nginx has almost a perfect correlation of 0.99 (in both Pearson and Spearman correlation). And, SQLite has a very strong correlation, with Pearson being 0.90 and Spearman 0.98. This signifies that configurations in nginx and SQLite have the same effect on their binary size as in their number of gadgets. Next, xz has a very strong correlation, but not perfect, with Pearson being 0.85 and Spearman 0.83. This suggests that there are configurations that have a different effect on the binary size from that in the number of gadgets. On the other hand, x264 differs from the three other systems. It has a weak to medium, positive, correlation, with Pearson being 0.52 and Spearman 0.82. In this system, we noticed that there are several options in its configurations that increase its binary size but reduce the number of its gadgets.

Answer to RQ_2: These results show that the attack surface of a software system highly depends on its used compile-time options during its build. Based on four popular systems, changing the system's default configuration, it is more likely that its number of gadgets will get reduced (in 63% of the cases) than they will get increased (in 25% of the cases) or remain the same (in 12% of the cases). On average, by enabling/disabling new options, the attack surface will be reduced far more (25%) than that it will be increased (6%). Moreover, there is a weak (0.52) to almost perfect (0.99) Pearson correlation between the variation of binary size and the number of gadgets in a given system.

5.3   Influential Compile-Time Options (RQ_3)

Which Options Are the Most Influential in These Systems? To answer it, we did a detailed analysis of the effect of each compile-time option on the system's binary size and gadgets, which is described in Sect. 4.3. The results are as follows.

x264: As shown in Fig. 5 (right), --system-libx264 is by far the most important option for predicting gadgets in x264 (around 80% of the importance). However, the prediction of binary size involves much more options and interactions among --enable-debug, --enable-strip, --disable-lsmash, and --disable asm. That is, there are more influential options (and more interactions to capture through learning) for size than for gadgets. It partly explains why achieving low prediction errors with gadgets is easier than with size (further details are given in the companion web page). The options' effects we have learned also make sense: identified options are related to the compiler behavior or libraries linked to the binary.

nginx: The option --without-http is the most influential (feature importance greater than 0.85). It is quite intuitive since this option deactivates a major functionality. It should be noted that --without-http corresponds to a realistic usage, since nginx can be used as *e.g.,* a reverse proxy or to handle arbitrary TCP connections. However, the strong importance of --without-http tends to hide the fact that other options are actually influential w.r.t. size and gadgets. Looking at the decision tree[12], we can observe that many options are actually interacting with the option --without-http. Such interactions are actually needed to reach high accuracy. Our learning can retrieve options like --without-http_proxy_module, --with-stream, *etc.*. An expert can certainly intuit the positive or negative effect, but neither to quantify the strength of the effects nor to capture interactions with other configuration choices. Hence,

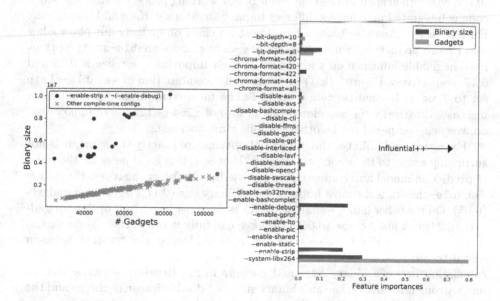

Fig. 5. An interaction example of two options in x264 that changes its binary size but not its number of gadgets (left). Feature importance in x264 (right)

---

[12] See https://github.com/diverse-project/confsurface/tree/main/nginx/nginx.pdf.

an expert can rely on the prediction model of `nginx` to explore configuration tradeoffs between functionality, size, and attack surface.

SQLite: Its most influential options are by far `--enable-all` and `--enable-fts5` with more than 90% of the importance. The importance of the first option is intuitive and its effect on binary size or gadgets is obvious since numerous features are added. The other option *"FTS5 is currently disabled by default for the source-tree configure script"*, but it *"is included as part of the* `SQLite` *amalgamation"*[13]. There are two other options `--enable-geopoly` and `--enable-session` that have an influence, but we observe very few interactions for binary size or gadgets. In summary, the *"take it all"* feature and the identification of an individual option (fts5) is sufficient to accurately configure `SQLite` w.r.t. size and gadgets.

xz: Compared to `SQLite`, the importance is more spread among compile-time options for `xz`. The maximum is 0.17 for binary size and 0.24 for gadgets, and there are 6 main influential options. We also observed many pair-wise interactions (*e.g.*, `--enable-sandbox` with `--enable-small`).

Are the Influential Options of a System the Same for Binary Size and Gadgets? We observed that the ways how options have an effect on the x264's binary size and gadgets differ, as shown in Fig. 5 (right). For instance, `--system-libx264` has a strong importance for gadgets (0.78), but its importance is much lower (0.18) for binary size. The intent of this option is to *"use system libx264 instead of internal"*. Hence, an interesting result of our learning process is that the way a code is integrated may have a different impact on attack surface and binary size. For instance, `--disable-lsmash` has almost no effect on gadgets but plays a key role in size prediction. Similarly, `--enable-debug` and `--enable-strip` options have negligible influence on gadgets while their importance for size is 0.19 and 0.17, respectively. Figure 5 (left) suggests that a combination of `--enable-strip` set to `True` and `--enable-debug` set to `False` for a compile-time configuration increases drastically the associated binary size of `x264` (+122.6% of binary size, on average, compared to the other compile-time options).

For `nginx` and `SQLite`, the influential options are exactly the same; it is not surprising owing to the strong correlation. However, it is good news for the reuse of prediction model and configuration knowledge. As for `xz`, however, the option `--enable-checks` is the most important for binary size (0.17), but not for gadgets (0.05). On the other hand, `--enable-small` is the most important option for gadgets (0.24) but not for size (0.05). We have carefully verified, there is no dependency and collinearity between these two options. Hence, the "switch" between `--enable-small` and `--enable-checks` mainly explains the strong but not perfect correlation between binary sizes and gadgets in `xz`. Besides, `--enable-checks` has a strong influence on the `xz`'s binary size, but disable integrity checks and the documentation[14] warns that *"this option should be used only when it is known*

---

[13] According to https://sqlite.org/fts5.html, last access February 2022.

[14] https://github.com/xz-mirror/xz/blob/master/INSTALL, last access February 2022.

to not cause problems". All these observations tend to show the complexity of configuring a system w.r.t. size, gadgets, and functionality.

Answer to RQ_3: Our learning process can identify influential options that make sense from a domain knowledge point of view. Moreover, our prediction model can be used to take informed decisions when customizing a software system at compile-time. We have also shown that options' effects and interactions on either binary size or gadgets can vary. As a user, it makes the tuning of software systems difficult to achieve at compile-time.

6   Discussion

In this section, we discuss our findings and share insights about the costs and benefits of learning the effects of compile-time configurations.

Costs. Findings from RQ_1, RQ_2, and RQ_3 show that knowing the precise effects of compile-time options is possible, but comes at a price. We noticed that there is a triple cost:

1. There is a *human cost* to automate the generation of a well-built system configuration. A configuration with a wrong combination of options, that have dependencies, usually triggers a warning or error during the system's build. Based on four systems, the options' dependencies are hardly documented. That is why we retrieved them manually when we build the feature models, requiring several tries and fixes. In addition, the provision of reusable containers with pre-installed libraries and tools (*e.g.,* Dockerfiles) can decrease the burden of developers, users, and researchers in charge of the building.
2. Then, to quantify the effects of each compile-time option on binary size and gadgets, but not only, the system needs to be built each time. But, this can be costly in terms of the *required time and disk resources*. For instance, the time to build x264 and NodeJS (another configurable system) in their default configuration varies between a few seconds and 30 min, respectively.
3. Lastly, there is also a smaller but important cost, the *learning cost*. Once the effects of options are measured and quantified, it is possible to instrument the different machine learning methods in order to obtain the final list of influential options and thus predict the best compile-time options to use w.r.t. user constraints. However, a tradeoff should be found between the accuracy of the learning and the time needed to train the models. For instance, in our case, *(i) random forest* is the most accurate and more stable, reaching low prediction errors with a relatively small number of compilations, *(ii) decision tree* is also competitive, less accurate but faster to train, whereas *(iii) linear regression* is both unstable and inaccurate[15].

---

[15] Detailed results about the tradeoff cost-accuracy of machine learning models can be consulted at https://github.com/diverse-project/confsurface/tree/main/learning/results.md.

Benefits. Despite these costs, having information about the effects of compile-time configuration space on the non-functional properties of a system is beneficial for different stakeholders. First, developers can use that knowledge to build and test only configurations with resolved dependencies and to find the best baseline configuration for users for which the system's binary size or security matters. It should be noted that the configuration knowledge about the binary size and surface attack is poorly documented in the four projects. This knowledge is also non-trivial: basic linear regression models are poorly accurate since interactions are not taken into account. In response, we are capable of synthesizing accurate information that is both interpretable and actionable to quantify the effects of options and their interactions. Developers can better document their projects and provide an infrastructure capable of building any configuration. Second, the identification of influential options (and interactions) will help users to have a quicker intuition on how to customize a given system in order to reach their purpose. Users can predict the properties of configurations without actually building them. An open issue is how to build tools (*e.g.,* configurators) on top of feature models and inferred knowledge to further assist users when configuring the compilation of their systems. In particular, we provided evidence that binary size and surface attack are not necessarily correlated and possibly conflicting. Beyond security and size concerns, there are other non-functional properties (*e.g.,* execution time) to consider, calling to explore tradeoffs and resolve multi-objective problems with automated guidance. We leave it as future work.

7   Threats to Validity

Internal Validity. A first internal threat stems from the installed external libraries in our environment, which resemble an instrumentation threat. In this study, we do not report on the version of the installed libraries in our experimentation environment, which are required by subject systems. We always installed the last possible version of each library. But, if our experiment is reproduced by installing an older or newer version of them then the resulting binary size, gadgets, and the effects of options may differ. For this reason, providing a Docker image to precisely reproduce our experiments is envisioned in our future work. It can also be useful for developers and maintainers. Another instrumentation threat is related to the manual identification of dependencies between compile-time options during the build of feature models for each subject system. New or other dependencies between compile-time options of the considered systems can be present, still, for all over 400 considered configurations per system, we make sure that the system is at least always compilable. Hence, on our next future step is to automatically identify the dependencies between compile-time options and to build the feature model of a given software system. A further internal threat is related to the sample of measurements used to test our prediction models. The sample may not be representative of the whole configuration space, which may threaten the supposed qualities of the models. To mitigate this threat, we use random sampling and compile hundreds of configurations. We also notice that the accuracy of learning models tends to reach a plateau with the increase of the training with no overfitting – it is a good signal.

External Validity. While we believe that the four selected subject systems from different application domains show the effect of compile-time options in two non-functional properties of typical configurable software systems, still, we considered only the C-based systems. Therefore, the considered number and used language of subject systems do not enable us to conclude that the results of a newly added system will always be in the same range as our obtained results.

8   Related Work

There are numerous works about the non-functional properties and performance of configurable systems (*e.g.,* see [6,10,13,18,23,24,27]). The idea is to build prediction models out of a sample of measurements. Non-functional properties are usually runtime performance (*e.g.,* execution time, memory consumption) that require the actual execution of the compiled system. In this work, we have considered non-functional properties that can be computed at compile-time, such as binary size and gadgets. Footprint has been subject to attention in [24] for Java-based and C-based systems. We have focused our effort on C-based projects with the ./configure facility. Our goal was to instrument a build infrastructure capable of compiling any configuration, making no assumptions about which options to consider or not. To the best of our knowledge, the effects of compile-time options on attack surface (gadgets) have not been considered in this context.

Halin *et al.* [7] built a testing scaffold for the entire configuration space of JHipster, a Web generator. They reported that building a variability-aware testing infrastructure requires a substantial engineering effort to cover all design, implementation and validation activities. We have shared similar difficulties for elaborating the FMs and anticipating all possible libraries required by any compile-time configuration (see Sect. 6). Our work can be seen as a re-engineering effort to make configurable ./configure. This is also an important topic in software product line engineering. Many techniques have been proposed to locate features, synthesize FMs out of artifacts, or recover an architecture out of variants [1,2,20,22,31]. In our study, we have started with a manual approach when recovering the informal documentation. Automated techniques come after to validate and refine both the FM and the build infrastructure.

There are several works in highly configurable systems that analyse the build files, such as Makefiles, of a system in order to extract its configuration or variability knowledge [17,30]. The main reason of these approaches is to detect the variability anomalies, such as dead code, that steams from Makefiles or during the build time of the system.

Xu *et al.* analyse over 600 real-world configuration issues in 4 subject systems to understand the consequences of too many configuration options (*a.k.a.,* knobs) [28]. They propose a way to simplify the configuration space of a system by removing, hiding, or categorizing them. Unlike them, we propose to configure a system by taking into consideration its binary size and attack surface.

9   Conclusion

Modern software systems are highly customizable through the compile-time options, which are especially extensive in C-based systems. These options are enabled or disabled during a system's build through the widely used `./configure`. While they have an evident impact on the functional properties of a system, their effect on its non-functional properties is hardly explored. In this work, we investigate the effect of compile-time options on the binary size and attack surface of a system by using four C-based systems. Our obtained results show that:

Depending on the used compile-time options in a configuration, the binary size and number of gadgets can be increased (244.13% and 30.08%, respectively) or decreased considerably (78.98% and 76.97%, respectively), compared to the baseline system configuration. Whereas, the variation of gadgets has a weak (0.52) to almost perfect (0.99) correlation to the binary size of a system.

Then, we show that the interactions among compile-time options can be best captured by expressive learning models. Our build infrastructure and learning process can accurately find the most influential options for binary size or gadgets. Our results show that developers and integrators can use prediction models to take informed decisions when configuring a system.

In short, practitioners can benefit from configuration knowledge that is nontrivial to quantify and otherwise undocumented. We will consider integrating configuration tools into these software projects to achieve size and attack surface goals, possibly with other (conflicting) functional or performance concerns. One lesson learned is that the computational and engineering cost of automating the exploration of the configuration space is not negligible and may be a barrier to the adoption of our approach for existing configurable projects. Modelling, reverse engineering, and learning techniques to assist developers in "scratching the surface" are therefore welcome. As future work, we plan to extend the study with more subjects, also implemented in other languages, and further consider compile-time options including compiler flags.

Acknowledgements. This research was funded by the SLIMFAST with DGA-Pôle Cyber (PEC) and Brittany region and the ANR-17-CE25-0010-01 VaryVary projects.

References

1. Assunção, W.K.G., Lopez-Herrejon, R.E., Linsbauer, L., Vergilio, S.R., Egyed, A.: Reengineering legacy applications into software product lines: a systematic mapping. Empir. Softw. Eng. **22**(6), 2972–3016 (2017). https://doi.org/10.1007/s10664-017-9499-z
2. Bécan, G., Acher, M., Baudry, B., Nasr, S.B.: Breathing ontological knowledge into feature model synthesis: an empirical study. Empir. Softw. Eng. **21**(4), 1794–1841 (2015). https://doi.org/10.1007/s10664-014-9357-1

3. Brown, M.D., Pande, S.: CARVE: practical security-focused software debloating using simple feature set mappings. In: Proceedings of the 3rd ACM Workshop on Forming an Ecosystem Around Software Transformation, pp. 1–7 (2019). https://doi.org/10.1145/3338502.3359764

4 Brown, M.D., Pande, S.: Is less really more? Towards better metrics for measuring security improvements realized through software debloating. In: 12th USENIX Workshop on Cyber Security Experimentation and Test (CSET 19) (2019). https://www.usenix.org/system/files/cset19-paper_brown.pdf

5. GNU: Autoconf - GNU Project. https://www.gnu.org/software/autoconf/

6. Guo, J., Czarnecki, K., Apel, S., Siegmund, N., Wąsowski, A.: Variability-aware performance prediction: a statistical learning approach. In: 2013 28th IEEE/ACM International Conference on Automated Software Engineering (ASE), pp. 301–311. IEEE (2013). https://doi.org/10.1109/ASE.2013.6693089

7. Halin, A., Nuttinck, A., Acher, M., Devroey, X., Perrouin, G., Baudry, B.: Test them all, is it worth it? Assessing configuration sampling on the JHipster Web development stack. Empir. Softw. Eng. **24**(2), 674–717 (2018). https://doi.org/10.1007/s10664-018-9635-4

8. Hampel, F.R., Ronchetti, E.M., Rousseeuw, P.J., Stahel, W.A.: Robust Statistics: The Approach Based on Influence Functions, vol. 196. Wiley (2011)

9. Herodotou, H., Lim, H., Luo, G., Borisov, N., Dong, L., Cetin, F.B., Babu, S.: Starfish: a self-tuning system for big data analytics. In: CIDR, vol. 11, pp. 261–272 (2011)

10. Jamshidi, P., Siegmund, N., Velez, M., Kästner, C., Patel, A., Agarwal, Y.: Transfer learning for performance modeling of configurable systems: an exploratory analysis. In: 2017 32nd IEEE/ACM International Conference on Automated Software Engineering (ASE), pp. 497–508. IEEE (2017). https://doi.org/10.1109/ASE.2017.8115661

11. Jiang, Y., Bao, Q., Wang, S., Liu, X., Wu, D.: RedDroid: android application redundancy customization based on static analysis. In: 2018 IEEE 29th International Symposium on Software Reliability Engineering (ISSRE), pp. 189–199. IEEE (2018). https://doi.org/10.1109/ISSRE.2018.00029

12. Kendall, M.G.: Rank Correlation Methods. Harvard Book, Harvard (1948)

13. Lesoil, L., Acher, M., Tërnava, X.H., Blouin, A., Jézéquel, J.M.: The interplay of compile-time and run-time options for performance prediction. In: Proceedings of the 25th ACM International Systems and Software Product Line Conference-Volume A, pp. 100–111 (2021). https://doi.org/10.1145/3461001.3471149

14. McGrenere, J., Moore, G.: Are we all in the same "bloat"? In: Proceedings of the Graphics Interface 2000 Conference, May 15–17, 2000, Montr'eal, Qu'ebec, Canada, pp. 187–196, May 2000. https://doi.org/10.20380/GI2000.25

15. Meinicke, J., Wong, C.P., Vasilescu, B., Kästner, C.: Exploring differences and commonalities between feature flags and configuration options. In: Proceedings of the ACM/IEEE 42nd International Conference on Software Engineering: Software Engineering in Practice, pp. 233–242 (2020). https://doi.org/10.1145/3377813.3381366

16. Molnar, C.: Interpretable Machine Learning (2020). Lulu.com

17. Nadi, S., Holt, R.: The Linux Kernel: a case study of build system variability. J. Softw. Evol. Process **26**(8), 730–746 (2014). https://doi.org/10.1002/smr.1595

18. Pereira, J.A., Acher, M., Martin, H., Jézéquel, J.M., Botterweck, G., Ventresque, A.: Learning software configuration spaces: a systematic literature review (2021). https://doi.org/10.1016/j.jss.2021.111044

19. Sayagh, M., Kerzazi, N., Adams, B., Petrillo, F.: Software configuration engineering in practice interviews, survey, and systematic literature review. IEEE Trans. Softw. Eng. **46**(6), 646–673 (2018). https://doi.org/10.1109/TSE.2018.2867847

20. Schlie, A., Knüppel, A., Seidl, C., Schaefer, I.: Incremental feature model synthesis for clone-and-own software systems in MATLAB/Simulink. In: Proceedings of the 24th ACM Conference on Systems and Software Product Line: Volume A-Volume A, pp. 1–12 (2020). https://doi.org/10.1145/3382025.3414973

21. Sharif, H., Abubakar, M., Gehani, A., Zaffar, F.: TRIMMER: application specialization for code debloating. In: Proceedings of the 33rd ACM/IEEE International Conference on Automated Software Engineering, pp. 329–339 (2018). https://doi.org/10.1145/3238147.3238160

22. She, S., Lotufo, R., Berger, T., Wąsowski, A., Czarnecki, K.: Reverse engineering feature models. In: Proceedings of the 33rd International Conference on Software Engineering, pp. 461–470 (2011). https://doi.org/10.1145/1985793.1985856

23. Siegmund, N., Grebhahn, A., Apel, S., Kästner, C.: Performance-influence models for highly configurable systems. In: Proceedings of the 2015 10th Joint Meeting on Foundations of Software Engineering, pp. 284–294 (2015). https://doi.org/10.1145/2786805.2786845

24. Siegmund, N., Rosenmüller, M., Kästner, C., Giarrusso, P.G., Apel, S., Kolesnikov, S.S.: Scalable prediction of non-functional properties in software product lines: footprint and memory consumption. Inf. Softw. Technol. **55**(3), 491–507 (2013). https://doi.org/10.1016/j.infsof.2012.07.020

25. Siegmund, N., Rosenmüller, M., Kuhlemann, M., Kästner, C., Apel, S., Saake, G.: SPL conqueror: toward optimization of non-functional properties in software product lines. Softw. Qual. J. **20**(3), 487–517 (2012). https://doi.org/10.1007/s11219-011-9152-9

26. Siegmund, N., Rosenmüller, M., Kuhlemann, M., Kästner, C., Saake, G.: Measuring non-functional properties in software product line for product derivation. In: 2008 15th Asia-Pacific Software Engineering Conference, pp. 187–194. IEEE (2008). https://doi.org/10.1109/APSEC.2008.45

27. Temple, P., Galindo, J.A., Acher, M., Jézéquel, J.M.: Using machine learning to infer constraints for product lines. In: Proceedings of the 20th International Systems and Software Product Line Conference, pp. 209–218 (2016). https://doi.org/10.1145/2934466.2934472

28. Xu, T., Jin, L., Fan, X., Zhou, Y., Pasupathy, S., Talwadker, R.: Hey, you have given me too many knobs!: understanding and dealing with over-designed configuration in system software. In: Proceedings of the 2015 10th Joint Meeting on Foundations of Software Engineering, pp. 307–319 (2015). https://doi.org/10.1145/2786805.2786852

29. Yin, Z., Ma, X., Zheng, J., Zhou, Y., Bairavasundaram, L.N., Pasupathy, S.: An empirical study on configuration errors in commercial and open source systems. In: Proceedings of the Twenty-Third ACM Symposium on Operating Systems Principles, pp. 159–172 (2011). https://doi.org/10.1145/2043556.2043572

30. Zhou, S., Al-Kofahi, J., Nguyen, T.N., Kästner, C., Nadi, S.: Extracting configuration knowledge from build files with symbolic analysis. In: 2015 IEEE/ACM 3rd International Workshop on Release Engineering, pp. 20–23. IEEE (2015). https://doi.org/10.1109/RELENG.2015.15

31. Ziadi, T., Frias, L., da Silva, M.A.A., Ziane, M.: Feature identification from the source code of product variants. In: 2012 16th European Conference on Software Maintenance and Reengineering, pp. 417–422. IEEE (2012). https://doi.org/10.1109/CSMR.2012.52

Nemo: A Tool to Transform Feature Models with Numerical Features and Arithmetic Constraints

Daniel-Jesus Munoz[1,2]([⊠]) [iD], Jeho Oh[3],
Monica Pinto[1,2] [iD], Lidia Fuentes[1,2] [iD], and Don Batory[3]

[1] ITIS Software, Universidad de Málaga, Málaga, Spain
[2] CAOSD, Departamento LCC, Universidad de Málaga, Andalucía Tech,
Málaga, Spain
{danimg,pinto,lff}@lcc.uma.es
[3] Department of Computer Science, University of Texas at Austin, Austin, TX, USA
{jeho,batory}@cs.utexas.edu

Abstract. Real-world *Software Product Lines* (SPLs) need *Numerical Feature Models* (NFMs) whose features not only have boolean values satisfying boolean constraints, but also have numeric attributes satisfying arithmetic constraints. A key operation on NFMs finds near-optimal performing products, which requires counting the number of SPL products. Typical constraint satisfaction solvers perform poorly on counting.

Nemo (Numbers, features, models) supports NFMs by *bit-blasting*, the technique that encodes arithmetic as boolean clauses. Nemo translates NFMs to propositional formulas whose products can be counted efficiently by #SAT solvers, enabling near-optimal products to be found. We evaluate Nemo with a diverse set of real-world NFMs, complex arithmetic constraints, and counting experiments in this paper.

Keywords: Feature model · Bit-blasting · Propositional formula · Numerical features · Model counting · Software product lines

1 Introduction

Software Product Line (SPL) engineering is a key reuse approach to build highly-configurable systems [1]. An SPL reduces the overall engineering effort to produce similar products by capitalizing on their commonalities and managing their configurations. A classical *Feature Model* (FM) defines SPL variability by boolean-valued features and boolean constraints, called *propositional formulas* (PFs). A PF is a relationship among features, where the presence or absence of some features requires or precludes other features. A valid combination of features is a *configuration* [2,5].

Real-world SPLs need *Numerical Feature Models* (NFMs). An example is the SPL of Linux repositories where packages have versioning and other numerical

© Springer Nature Switzerland AG 2022
G. Perrouin et al. (Eds.): ICSR 2022, LNCS 13297, pp. 59–75, 2022.
https://doi.org/10.1007/978-3-031-08129-3_4

attributes [29] called *Numerical Features* (NFs). Relationships among NFs are arithmetic constraints. In effect, NFMs are FMs with NFs.

SAT solvers find configurations of FMs, because FMs can be translated to PFs, and SAT is efficient for finding PF solutions (ie., configurations). Unfortunately, SAT performs poorly on counting as it enumerates products, which is infeasible for large SPL product spaces, $\gg 10^6$ products [30].

Why is counting important? Because counting products enables unbiased statistical inferences on large product spaces [21,28]. That, in turn, can be used to find the best performing configuration in a user-constrained SPL product space given a defined workload [28,39].

Only a handful of automated solvers support NFMs, namely *Satisfiability Modulo Theories* (SMT) [4] and *Constraint Programming* (CP) [34] solvers. Unfortunately, SMT and CP solvers cannot count and instead perform brute-force enumeration. In contrast, *#SAT* solvers extend SAT solvers to count the number of solutions of a PF efficiently without enumeration [9]. #SAT solvers outperform SMT and CP solvers on counting. We use techniques to translate NFMs into PFs [26]. Concretely, *bit-blasting* [11] encodes numerical values into bits and arithmetic constraints into PFs.

In this paper, we present Nemo (<u>N</u>umbers, <u>fe</u>atures, <u>mo</u>dels) which natively supports NFMs and efficient SAT operations to find NFM products (satisfying boolean and/or arithmetic constraints) as well as #SAT counting NFM products. Nemo's NFM language is simple; it supports constant, enumerated, and range variables, along with boolean and arithmetic constraints. Given an NFM, Nemo generates a PF in the standard format for SAT-based tools. At which point, a SAT or #SAT tool can be invoked.

The novel contributions of our paper are:

- Explaining how Nemo automatically translates and optimizes the encoding of arithmetic operations (as complex as multiplication, division, and modulo) and arithmetic constraints on NFs into PFs; and
- Experimentally comparing the run-time of Nemo with popular SMT and CP solvers on processing bit-blasted PFs on artificial NFMs and 7 real-world NFMs with up to 10^{45} configurations using (1) benchmarks for arithmetic expressions and (2) benchmarks for counting tasks.

Nemo is open-source: https://github.com/danieljmg/Nemo_tool.

2   Background

2.1   Propositional Formulas of Feature Models

A classical feature model uses only boolean features but this very restriction allows it to be transformed into a PF, where features are boolean variables and constraints are clauses [2,5]. State-of-the-art tools that convert feature models into PFs are FeatureIDE [41] and Glencoe [35]; both translate a graphically-drawn feature model into a PF in a *Conjunctive Normal Form* (CNF).

However, real-world SPLs use NFMs that contain both binary features and NFs [17]. An NF has a name N, a type (ie., domain), and range (eg., N ∈ [1, 2, ...128]). NFMs add arithmetic constraints to the set of propositional connectives. And arithmetic constraints can constrain boolean features and vice-versa.

Two examples of NFMs are: (1) the HADAS eco-assistant [27] where energy parameters are represented as NFs in an integer domain, and propositional connectives and inequalities are present in cross-tree constraints (eg., AEScrypto ⇒ keySize>128) and (2) WeaFQAs [18] has integer and float attributes with propositional connectives and interval constraints (ie., numerical value ranges).

2.2 Bit-Blasting

Bit-blasting, also called *flattening*, is the transformation of a bit-vector arithmetic formula to a PF [3]. Variables are bit-vectors and arithmetic operations are propositional clauses that reference bits. The resulting PF is satisfiable whenever the original formula is. Our work focuses on basic arithmetic relations and operations, and of course, counting. We present operations in order of their usage frequency in real-world NFMs [26]: equality (=), inequalities ($\neq$, >, $\geq$), addition (+), subtraction (-), multiplication (∗), division (/), and modulo (%).

3 Bit-Blasting Basic Arithmetic Operations

The main property of bit-vectors is their width which defines: a) the minimum and maximum limits of the original numerical variables, and b) if the vector is unsigned (ie., binary *sign-magnitude* encoding) or signed (ie., binary *two's complement* encoding). We use the Big-Endian representation where the first bit of the bit-vector encodes the sign as positive (0) or negative (1).

Table 1 shows examples of two's complement bit-blasting PFs for arithmetic relations on Big-Endian signed integers with a value range of [-4,3] (ie., n = 3 bits) where bit-1 is the integer sign:

$$a, b = < a_1, a_2, \ldots a_n >, < b_1, b_2, \ldots b_n > \quad \bigwedge \quad \text{where } a_i, b_i \in \{0, 1\}; 1 \leq i \leq n$$

Of course, we could have used larger widths in Table 1, but n = 3 is sufficient to grasp the encoding patterns. Equality (==) is the conjunction of bitwise equivalences (row 1, col PF). Inequality ($\neq$) is a bit-by-bit disjunction of XORs ($\oplus$) (row 2, col PF). After the numerical sign comparison (first clause of col PF in rows 3 and 4), there are bit-by-bit equivalences until the last bit of the series, which involve an implication in case of $\geq$ (row 4, col 3), or a disjunction of opposites in case of > (row 3, col 3).

Arithmetic encoding patterns are more complex. Addition and multiplication of bit-vectors can produce a result outside the domain range. For example, for 3 signed bits, if we perform '3+1', the result is '4', for which we need 4 signed bits. The extra bit is called a *carry bit*. Then, a binary addition requires two data inputs and produces two outputs, the sum S of the equation and a carry bit C as

Table 1. Propositional formulas for 3-bit two's complement signed integers

Row	Operation	Bit-Blasted Model	Propositional Formula
1	$(NF_a == NF_b)$	$(a_1 == b_1) \wedge (a_2 == b_2) \wedge (a_3 == b_3)$	$(a_1 \Leftrightarrow b_1) \wedge (a_2 \Leftrightarrow b_2) \wedge (a_3 \Leftrightarrow b_3)$
2	$(NF_a \neq NF_b)$	$(a_1 \neq b_1) \vee (a_2 \neq b_2) \vee (a_3 \neq b_3)$	$(a_1 \oplus b_1) \vee (a_2 \oplus b_2) \vee (a_3 \oplus b_3)$
3	$(NF_a > NF_b)$	$(a_1 < b_1) \vee ((a_1 == b_1) \wedge (a_2 > b_2)) \vee$ $((a_1 == b_1) \wedge (a_2 == b_2) \wedge (a_3 > b_3))$	$(\neg a_1 \wedge b_1) \vee ((a_1 \Leftrightarrow b_1) \wedge (a_2 \wedge \neg b_2)) \vee$ $((a_1 \Leftrightarrow b_1) \wedge (a_2 \Leftrightarrow b_2) \wedge (a_3 \wedge \neg b_3))$
4	$(NF_a \geq NF_b)$	$(a_1 < b_1) \vee ((a_1 == b_1) \wedge (a_2 \geq b_2)) \vee$ $((a_1 == b_1) \wedge (a_2 == b_2) \wedge (a_3 \geq b_3))$	$(\neg a_1 \wedge b_1) \vee ((a_1 \Leftrightarrow b_1) \wedge (b_2 \Rightarrow a_2)) \vee$ $((a_1 \Leftrightarrow b_1) \wedge (a_2 \Leftrightarrow b_2) \wedge (b_3 \Rightarrow a_3))$
5	$(NF_a \pm NF_b)$	$s_1^4 \equiv \quad [c_3, (a_1 \oplus b_1) \oplus c_2,$ $(a_2 \oplus b_2) \oplus c_1, (a_3 \oplus b_3) \oplus c_0]$ $c_i^3 \equiv \quad (a_i \wedge b_i) \vee c_{i-1}$ $c_0 \equiv \quad (`+' \Rightarrow 0) \wedge (`-' \Rightarrow 1)$	$[(a_3 \wedge b_3) \vee ((a_2 \wedge b_2) \vee ((a_1 \wedge b_1) \vee \pm)),$ $(a_1 \oplus b_1) \oplus ((a_2 \wedge b_2) \vee ((a_1 \wedge b_1) \vee \pm)),$ $(a_2 \oplus b_2) \oplus ((a_1 \wedge b_1) \vee \pm),$ $(a_3 \oplus b_3) \oplus \pm]$
6	$(NF_a * NF_b)$	$M \equiv \quad NF_a + NF_a \ldots + NF_a$ $\qquad \qquad |NF_b| \text{ times}$ $m_6 \equiv \quad a_1 \oplus b_1$	Too large to represent Apply addition (5th row) $|NF_b|$ times
7	(NF_a / NF_b)	$|NF_a| - |NF_b| - |NF_b| \ldots - |NF_b|$ $D \equiv \#\text{times penultimate negative value}$ $d_3 \equiv \quad a_1 \oplus b_1$	Too large to represent Apply subtraction (5th row) D times
8	$(NF_a \% NF_b)$	$|NF_a| - |NF_b| - |NF_b| \ldots - |NF_b|$ $MOD \equiv \text{penultimate negative value}$ $mod_3 \equiv \quad 0$	Too large to represent Apply subtraction (5th row) D (7th row) times

shown in the operation 5 of Table 1. Subtraction in a two's complement encoding is an addition with an opposite sign bit (ie., $c_0 = 1$). The multiplication pattern is described in row 6 of Table 1, which basically is a sign bit calculation plus a sequence of additions with a **double** bit-width. Division in row 7 is the times of the last but one subtraction of the second operand till the result is below zero. The modulo operation in row 8 is what is left after the division (ie., until we cannot subtract anymore keeping above zero). For multiplication and division, the sign is the XOR of the most significant bit of both operands (a_1 and b_1). The sign bit of the resulting modulo operation is always 0 (ie., modulo always returns a positive number).

The majority of SAT solvers primarily work with PFs in CNF [9]. Nemo applies the optimal alternative – Tseitin's CNF transformation with skolemization [43]. It is the fastest known encoding to transform PFs into a CNF formula while maintaining model equivalence and model count (ie., not altering the total number of solutions).

4 Nemo

Bit-blasting NFMs is a tough task to perform manually. The current prototype does it automatically including boolean and arithmetic features and constraints.

4.1   Prototype Overview

Figure 1 presents an overview of Nemo, in which a *modeling expert* defines an NFM for a given SPL. Nemo provides a simple language designed to support boolean and numerical variables and mixed constraints NFMs, concretely:

- Features of domain *Boolean*, *Integer* and *Natural* (by default);
- *Constant* and *Enumerated* features, and *Ranges* of values;
- *Cardinality-based*, *Mandatory* and *Optional* (by default) features;
- *Propositional Logic*: equivalences, implications, negations, conjuctions, disjunctions, parenthetical expressions, etc..;
- *Inequalities*: equal, not equal, greater (or equal), lower (or equal); and
- *Arithmetic*: addition, subtraction, multiplication, division, and modulo.

The input to Nemo is a `.txt` file. The Nemo transformation procedure is explained in Algorithm 1.

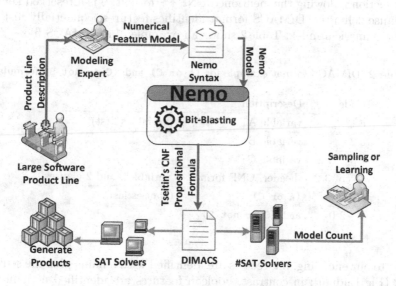

Fig. 1. Nemo tool usage overview. (Color figure online)

Algorithm 1: Nemo Complete Procedure (blue lines of Fig. 1)

Input: NFM defined in a `.txt` file
1 Parse features names;
2 Calculate features types;
3 Calculate NFs bit-widths;
4 Optimize and register the declared and calculated constraints;
5 Bit-blast the NFM;
6 Transform the bit-blasted NFM into a PF;
7 Transform the PF into its Tseitin CNF form;
8 Transform the Tseitin CNF PF into DIMACS;
Result: DIMACS file of the bit-blasted NFM

The default output of Nemo is an NFM transformed into a PF in DIMACS format. DIMACS dates back to 1993 and is the de-facto input format standard for SAT solvers.[1] A DIMACS CNF file has three parts: an optional comment section with the prefix `c`, a mandatory problem line with the prefix `p`, and the clauses section following the mentioned CNF PF format. 0 is a reserved keyword for a clause delimiter. DIMACS format identifies features sequentially just with a unique numerical index. Table 2 shows an example of a DIMACS file:

Table 2. DIMACS format example for `(A or C) and (C or not B)` formula

Code	Description	
c 1	variable A	(variables first)
c 2	variable B	
c 3	variable C	
p cnf 3 2	header, CNF format, 3 variables, and 2 clauses	
1 3 0	`(A or C)`	(clauses last)
3 −2 0	`and (C or not B)`	

Due to our encoding, bit-vectors are identified with a name plus the sequence of bits (Big Endian); in contrast, boolean features are identified as name plus *Boolean* keyword. **Note:** A CNF Tseitin transformation of a bit-blasted NFM generates extra variables. Table 3 shows a bit-blasted example in DIMACS. As shown in Fig. 1, the generated DIMACS file can then be used to generate products with a SAT solver, or to count configurations with a #SAT solver. The latter is useful for fast probabilistic sampling and learning [32].

4.2 Numerical Feature Modeling in Nemo

Currently, most SPL feature modeling languages are tool-specific [33], eg., Clafer [6]. For Nemo, we abstract the notion of NFMs defining just two entities as in [24]:

---

[1] DIMACS: http://archive.dimacs.rutgers.edu/pub/challenge/satisfiability.

Table 3. Nemo output for expr: `(A = B) requires C; A,B ∈ [−1,1], C Boolean`

Code	Description
c 1	Abit1
c 2	Abit2
c 3	Bbit1
c 4	Bbit2
c 5	Tseitin1
c 6	Tseitin2
c 7	Tseitin3
c 8	C Boolean
p cnf 8 14	header, cnf format, 8 variables, and 14 clauses
−2 0	not Abit2
−4 0	not Bbit2
−2 −4 −5 0	and (not Abit2 or not Bbit2 or not Tseitin1)
2 4 −5 0	and (Abit2 or Bbit2 or not Tseitin1)
2 −4 5 0	and (Abit2 or not Bbit2 or Tseitin1)
−2 4 5 0	and (not Abit2 or Bbit2 or Tseitin1)
−1 −3 −6 0	and (not Abit1 or not Bbit1 or not Tseitin2)
1 3 −6 0	and (Abit1 or Bbit1 or not Tseitin2)
1 −3 6 0	and (Abit1 or not Bbit1 or Tseitin2)
3 −1 6 0	and (Bbit1 or not Abit1 or Tseitin2)
−6 7 0	and (not Tseitin2 or Tseitin3)
−5 7 0	and (not Tseitin1 or Tseitin3)
5 6 −7 0	and (Tseitin1 or Tseitin2 or not Tseitin3)
8 7 0	and (C or Tseitin3)

generic variables and functions. Then, following the meta-model of [19], we can define a NFM as a formula with different domains, where a variable is a feature and a function is a hierarchical relationship or constraint. For that, we decided to define a keywords-based syntax for our first prototype. Our motivation was to reduce Nemo's learning curve. Consequently, we used a cheat sheet:

- `def Var_Name D` defines a named feature with D as its domain or range;
- `bool`, `integer` and `natural` (ie., natural numbers or positive integers) are the supported domains;
- `[X]` indicates a constant feature with a value X;
- `[X:Y]` indicates a range between X and Y inclusive;
- `[X,Y,Z]` indicates an enumerated type with restricted values X, Y or Z;
- `and`/`or` are the conjunctions and disjunctions;
- `<->`/`->`/`neg` are equivalences, implications and negations;
- `=`/`>`/`<`/`>=`/`<=`/`!=` are the equalities/inequalities; and
- `+`/`−`/`*`/`/`/`%` are the numerical operators.

Listing 1.1 illustrates most of the types of supported clauses:

```
def  A_constant  [3]
def  B_natural  [0:3]
def  C_natural_2  [:3]
def  D_integer  [-2:1]
def  E_enumerated_integer  [-1, 2, 4, 8]
def  F_new_Boolean  bool  0
def  G_predefined_Boolean  bool  23
ct   G_predefined_Boolean  or  F_new_Boolean
ct   ((A_constant * B_natural) > C_natural) ->
     (F_new_Boolean or (E_enumerated_integer = D_integer))
```

Listing 1.1. A Nemo NFM: (G or F) and ((A*B)>C) requires (F or (E = D))

Sequentially, the above means:

1. A_constant: a constant **natural** NF with a value of 3;
2. B_natural: a **natural** NF between 0 and 3;
3. C_natural_2: a **natural** NF between 0 and 3,
4. D_integer: an integer NF between -2 and 1 in two's complement encoding;
5. E_enumerated_integer: an enumerated integer NF with exactly 4 values;
6. F_new_Boolean: a boolean feature. Zero (0) means that it is a new feature;
7. G_predefined_Boolean: a boolean feature defined in a previous DIMACS NFM where 23 is that feature identifier in the original NFM;
8. A boolean parenthetical propositional expression: (G or F); and
9. An arithmetic constraint: ((A*B)>C) requires (F or (E = D)).

We have two tags for the objects: def are feature declarations and ct are their constraints. The format is flexible, allowing any tag at any line. Range definitions can have one of the limits omitted (eg., [: 3] is considered as [0 : 3]).

4.3   Implementation of Smart Transformations

Nemo is a cross-platform tool developed in Python 3.10.8 x86_64. We tackled several engineering challenges in its implementation.

First, Nemo dynamically sets a feature as a **natural** or an **integer**, as the bit-blasted encoding of some operations are different (ie., inequalities, division, and modulo).[2] If any value of a NF is negative, it is considered an **integer**.

Second, Nemo dynamically calculates the minimum bit-width of each NF to generate the shortest PF. The process is based on the possible values of each NF (eg., range, enumeration) and the domain; **natural** NFs and constraints produce smaller PFs. For instance, the most optimal encoding for an enumerated feature with just two values (eg., -1 and 9), and that is not involved in arithmetic expressions, is a single bit **natural** NF.

---

[2] Besides inequalities, division, and modulo, arithmetic operations do not make unsigned/signed distinction due to the Two's complement encoding.

Third, Nemo readjusts the previous computed widths based on NFM constraints. Leaving aside boolean features, every NF involved in operations with other NFs must have the same type and bit-width in order to apply bit-blasting. Our solution was to recursively search for the NF with the highest bit-width of each set of NFs involved in a constraint, and set that bit-width to the rest of the features sharing a constraint. For instance, transforming a `natural` into an `integer` NF, is to add one bit for the sign.

Fourth, Nemo readjusts bit-widths in case of mathematical operations that can produce extra carry-bits. The most efficient is to define the highest from:

- **Addition:** Extending one bit for the first addition, followed by extra bits per sets of two extra additions. For example, A + B + C + D = E needs two extra carry bits. Note that `natural` numerical ranges are up to $2^{bit-width}-1$.
- **Multiplication:** The extended bit-width is the original multiplied by the number of multiplication operands plus 1. For instance, A * B * C = D implies that $bit\text{-}width_{updated} = (bit\text{-}width_{current} \times 3)+1$.

4.4 Nemo **Optimizations by Pre-processing the** NFM

Bit-blasting and Tseitin transformations create different size CNF PFs depending on the equation. Nemo takes advantage of that by replacing and adjusting constraints to produce shorter PFs. Concretely:

1. $>$/$<$/$+$/$-$ do not create extra variables;
2. $\geq$/$\leq$ create $(bit\text{-}width-1)$ Tseitin variables in the NFs involved;
3. $=$ creates $(bit\text{-}width)$ Tseitin variables in the NFs involved;
4. $\neq$ creates $(bit\text{-}width+1)$ Tseitin variables in the NFs involved;
5. $/$ creates $(3\times2^{bit-width\,-1})$ Tseitin variables in the NFs involved;
6. $\%$ creates $(14\times2^{bit-width\,-1})$ Tseitin variables in the NFs involved; and
7. $*$ creates $(6^{bit-width\,-1})$ Tseitin variables in the NFs involved.

The only two operations naturally replaceable by an alternative with a shorter PF encoding are $\{\geq,\ \leq\}$ by $\{>,<\}$ respectively. (eg., A $\geq$ 1 and A $\leq$ 2 are equivalent to A $>$ 0 and A $<$ 3). Additionally, Nemo removes duplicated constraints. For example, in case of the constraints A $<$ 2 and A $<$ 1 the first one is redundant. Finally, Nemo dynamically prioritizes `natural` NFs, as unsigned operations are more scalable – need smaller bit-widths and produce smaller PFs.

5   Evaluation

We answer the following research questions to evaluate Nemo:

RQ1: Are Nemo bit-blasted NFMs viable for any bit-width?
RQ2: Do Nemo bit-blasted NFMs allow faster counting?

RQ1 evaluates the viability of Nemo for different NFM constraints with increasing bit-widths. **RQ2** evaluates how Nemo performs compared to state-of-art SMT and CP solvers for large real-world SPLs. To count the number of configurations of Nemo bit-blasted NFMs, we used `sharpSAT` [42], the state-of-the-art model counter for PFs. Every test has been carried out on an Intel(R) Core i7-4790 CPU@3.60 GHz processor with 16 GB of memory RAM and an SSD running an up-to-date Lubuntu 20.04 LTS X86_64.

RQ1: **Are** Nemo **bit-blasted** NFMs **viable for any bit-width?**

We start analyzing the most complex types of NFM operations – arithmetic. Additionally, we add the least complex inequality (i.e., =), which allows us to focus on arithmetic equalities. For similar reasons, we opted for `natural` instead of `integer` NFs. The first set of 5 NFM constraints that were analyzed are defined by ((A op B) = C) where op $\in \{+, -, *, /, \%\}$ from now on.

Formulas with different bit-widths (#b) from 2 up to 16 step 2 were generated. Remember that the maximum bit-width, as said earlier, is limited to the most demanding operation. Finally, if counting surpasses 15 minutes we considered it a *time-out* due to a high probability of never finishing. For each expression, we measured: a) the number of CNF clauses generated in each PF, and b) the time in seconds to count the configurations of those PFs with `sharpSAT`.

Figure 2 shows in two graphs the first results. The X-axis are bit-vector widths, and the Y-axis is the number of generated clauses or counting time in seconds respectively. As operation * counting timed-out, we scale the graphs up to bit-width 16. It is worth noting that Fig. 2 was truncated at 16-bits, even though addition (+) did not time-out even when the bit-width was 40.

- Number of clauses: + and − linearly grow in direct proportion with the bit-width. / and % almost linearly grow at 2× rate. * grows exponentially.
- Time to count: + and − linearly grow in proportion with the bit-width, keeping below a second for 16 bit-width. *, / and % grow exponentially, keeping below 50 s for 12 bit-width.

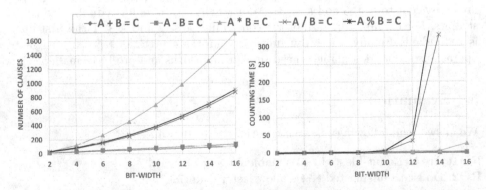

Fig. 2. Nemo generated clauses and counting time in seconds of arithmetic operations.

As the number of NF variables is proportional to the bit-width, Tseitin's transformation guarantees a linear increase O(3n+1) [43]. As operation * creates (2*bit-width) carry-bits, Tseitin's transformation increase is negligible. Hence, carry-bits are the ones causing the exponential growth.[3]

Further, we analyze logic and arithmetic mixed nested constraints, and up to four conjuncted numerical constraints. Following the previous procedure, we prioritize the fewer demanding operations (ie., =, +, ⇒) to reduce interactions for cleaner insights. The second set of 4 constraints analyzed are:

1. ((A + B) = C) ⇒ D
2. (A + B) = C
3. (A + B) = C ∧ (D + E) = F
4. ((A + B) = C)∧((D + E) = F)∧((G + H) = I)∧((J + K) = L)

Figure 3 shows the second set of results. Again, the number of clauses is linearly proportional to the bit-width and the number of operations and constraints. Boolean operations needed fewer clauses than arithmetic operations. While nesting did not especially affect the number of clauses, it caused an exponential increase in counting time including a 12 bit-width time-out.

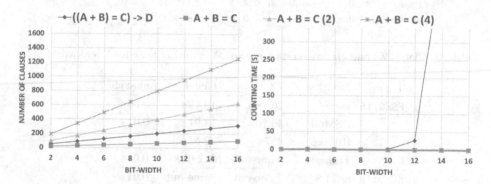

Fig. 3. Nemo generated clauses and counting time in seconds of sets of equations.

Nemo **natural** encoding was feasible up to a 12 bit-width. While multiplication is the only exponential transformation, division, modulo, and nesting are the slowest to count; we suggest discretizing their numerical ranges, keeping them within 12 bit-width for the current prototypes of Nemo and **sharpSAT**.

Conclusion: Nemo NFs are unbounded by default, but its encoding scales up to 12 bit-width per number with a counting time under 10 s. The number of clauses is indirectly related to that time. Division, modulo, and nesting are the slowest constraints to count.

---

[3] Multiplying two bit-vectors could generate a double width one (eg., $2^3 * 2^3 = 2^6$). Those are many carry-bits compared to additions which create a maximum of one.

RQ2: Do Nemo bit-blasted NFMs allow faster counting?

We expect **RQ1** counting conclusions to be an upper-bound for other solvers as larger bit-widths imply more configurations to analyze, which sometimes becomes exponential. We used 7 real-world NFMs obtained from [29,37]. Table 4 lists them, where each system has a different number of NFs and/or different configuration space size. Henceforth, we use FSE2015 to denote the FMs from [37]. We modeled their NFMs independently in Clafer, Z3, and Nemo syntax, and additionally ran Nemo to generate the PFs just for sharpSAT. Considering the bottleneck found in **RQ1**, if a NF is unbounded or surpasses $[0, 2^{12}-1]$, it is limited to 2^{12} options for the 3 solvers, which implies values discretization within some of the NFMs (eg., we can represent the even values of $[0, 2^{13}]$ in 12 bits).

Table 4. List of models with numerical features and constraints

Type	NFM	Description	#F	#NFs	#Configs	Benchmark
FSE2015	Dune	Multi-grid solver	11	3	2,304	Equation solving times
	HSMGP	Stencil-grid solver	14	3	3,456	
	HiPAcc	Image processing	33	2	13,485	
	Trimesh	Triangle mesh library	13	4	239,360	
KConfig	axTLS	Client-server library	94	9	4.96×10^{38}	Build sizes
	Fiasco	Real-time microkernel	234	5	3.06×10^{12}	
	uClibc-ng	C library	269	6	8.20×10^{45}	

Table 5. Clafer, Z3 and Nemo encoding sharpSAT counting time for 7 real-world SPLs

Type	Model	Z3	Clafer	sharpSAT
FSE2015	Dune	26.18 s	10.49 s	0.01 s
	HSMGP	40.70 s	13.91 s	0.01 s
	HiPAcc	457 s	32.52 s	0.01 s
	Trimesh	Time-out	217.01 s	0.01 s
KConfig	axTLS	Time-out	Time-out	0.01 s
	Fiasco	Time-out	Time-out	0.01 s
	uClibc-ng	Time-out	Time-out	0.01 s

We compared for the same number of solutions the time to count them in seconds with sharpSAT, and one CP and SMT solvers: Clafer[4] and Z3[5] respectively. Z3 and Clafer do not strictly perform model counting as sharpSAT does, instead they enumerate by: 1) deriving a configuration, 2) making the negation of that solution as a constraint, and 3) repeating steps 1 and 2 until the constrained model is unsatisfiable.[6,7] If counting took more than 15 min, we considered it a

---

[4] Clafer: https://www.clafer.org/.

[5] Z3py: https://github.com/Z3Prover/z3.

[6] Z3 developer on model counting: https://github.com/Z3Prover/z3/issues/934.

[7] Clafer Choco solver: https://github.com/chocoteam/choco-solver/blob/master/src/main/java/org/chocosolver/solver/search/strategy/Search.java.

time-out. Table 5 lists the results. In summary, sharpSAT counted NFMs configurations in under 0.01 s where Z3 and Clafer timed-out for KConfig models. This empirically demonstrates the superior speed of algorithms for model counting versus enumerating.

Conclusion: sharpSAT counts the configurations of Nemo *PFs considerably faster than Z3 and Clafer do with native* NFMs*.*

6   Nemo Tool Scalability and Threats to Validity

In **RQ1** we tested the scalability of counting with sharpSATthe bit-blasted models generated by Nemo. In this section, we use the same NFMs to test the scalability of the transformation process itself. In other words, we now evaluate Nemo's runtime. We present the results in Fig. 4, and although there are two tools performing different tasks, we infer similar conclusions. Nemo finishes *instantly* for addition and subtraction operations. However, the runtime time is slightly exponential for division and modulo, and truly exponential for multiplication, due to the carry bits of the operations. Nevertheless, all transformations finished below 40 min for a 16 bit-width. Regarding nested and stacked constraints, it takes a maximum of 85 s to process all equalities. Comparing Fig. 2 and Fig. 4, there is clear relationship between Nemo transformation time and the number of clauses of that transformation. This scalability issue was theoretically predicted [11].

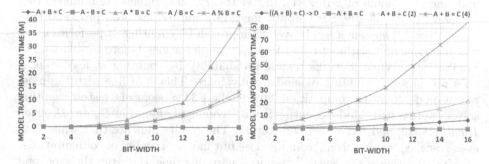

Fig. 4. Nemo runtime in seconds of arithmetic operations and equations sets.

Internal Validity. To control randomness, we conducted 97 experiments and averaged the results for a confidence level of 95% with a 10% margin of error [40]. For **RQ2**, we used the counting methods that are proposed by the developers of each solver: sharpSAT is the default execution, Clafer requires the noprint option, and Z3 requires a counting loop.

External Validity. We used the 7 real-world SPLs of Table 4 which have different numbers of features, domains, and constraints. For complex constraints, synthetic models were evaluated. While we are aware that our results may not generalize to all SPLs, their trends are identical in different cases. Similarly, although being state-of-the-art, Z3 and Clafer may not be representative of all

SMT and CP solvers. Additionally, a manual bit-blasting approach for NFs and basic operations was successfully applied for counting-based optimizations of SPLs [26]. Our work extends the encoding to complete arithmetic, and creates a tool that allows NFMs modeling while automatizing and optimizing all the process.

7   Related Work

Work tackling NFMs is rare [22]. Some considered NFs as classical features with just present/absent states [8,15,29]. Some encoded NFs as alternative features, where each value of a NF was considered a distinct feature [20]. Shi [36] used a single type of feature called 'pseudo-boolean' with only Successor (+1) and Predecessor (-1) operations. In [7], each boolean feature had related attributes – a set of variables in the form (name, value, domain). However, attributes and NFs are essentially different: attributes are not nodes of the variability tree, and as opposed to a NF, a change in the value of an attribute does not result in a different configuration [25]. Hence, counting the size of a product space will return a lower-than-expected value.

SMT and CP solvers natively support representation and reasoning of NFMs. However, #CP or #SMT solvers, counting generalizations of CP and SMT, are nonexistent. This is to be expected, as CP and SMT theories are unbounded by default [31], being unaware of allocated memory or domain definitions (eg., undefined maximum of x in x$\geq$1). In SAT theory, all variables are bounded (ie., boolean). Consequently, SMT approximation counting has been proposed [14]. STP solver [16] implements a bit-vector approach for counting. It performs array optimizations and arithmetic and Boolean simplifications before bit-blasting to MiniSat [38]. While it works to test satisfiability by counting at least one, it does not preserve counting or model equivalence. This is in line with the most recent model counting competition (2020), where 34 versions of 8 fastest counting solvers were tested. Model counting is more commonly found in *Binary Decision Diagrams* [12] and SAT-based [42] solvers. The results indicate that while fast, even so-called 'exact solvers' count a close but inexact number of configurations.

Simplification of NFMs usually reduces reasoning time. However, those beyond the ones implemented in Nemo do not preserve counting or model equivalence [13]. Nevertheless, the bit-width bottleneck is shared even in solutions that perform approximate counting. An example is Boolector reasoner [10], which lazily instantiates array axioms and macros. Even Z3 [23] applies bit-blasting to every operation besides equality, which are, then, handled by a specific algorithms.

8   Conclusions and Future Work

The size of an SPL configuration space grows exponentially with an increasing number of features. Compared to classical FMs, NFMs have more complex relationships due to larger domains (natural and integer) and more complex types of constraints (ie., arithmetic). That makes techniques of statistical reasoning and learning that much more important to understand and support, where a key reasoning operation is model counting. Unfortunately, while automated solvers can analyze NFMs, they were not developed with the objective of counting configurations. Again, counting configurations is key to finding near optimal SPL configurations (eg., find one of the top configurations minimizing the run-time of a given benchmark [26,28,32]).

We developed Nemo, a prototype that automatically optimizes and transforms NFMs to a Tseitin PF in DIMACS format. Nemo represents NFs as bit-vectors by means of bit-blasting, while arithmetic constraints are encoded as propositional clauses. We evaluated Nemo by transforming different synthetic and real-world NFMs to PFs and used existing SAT-based approaches to count configurations. We have shown that Nemo can:

- model, automatically optimize, and transform NFMs by using the Nemo language;
- use bit-blasting to encode common types of numerical features and arithmetic constraints;
- represent NFMs up to 12 bit-width of accuracy without overhead for almost every combination of boolean and arithmetical operations;
- use **sharpSAT** to count the number of configurations up to 10^{45} products in under 0.01 s. Analyzing a 10^{45} product space is infeasible with current state-of-the-art SMT and CP solvers as they count by enumeration.

We are confident our work can support statistical and learning techniques that analyze NFMs of real-world SPLs. Our research also suggests future explorations:

- bit-blast more features of other domains and with new types of relationships (eg., strings with concatenation and sub-string operations);
- optimize the transformation to generate models that are faster to count;
- run Nemo in an ecosystem with different solvers with extended support (eg., attributes, graphical interface); and
- beautify Nemo's language to be a more human-friendly modeling language.

Acknowledgement. Munoz, Pinto and Fuentes work is supported by the European Union's H2020 research and innovation programme under grant agreement DAEMON 101017109, by the projects co-financed by FEDER funds LEIA UMA18-FEDERJA-15, MEDEA RTI2018-099213-B-I00 and Rhea P18-FR-1081 and the PRE2019-087496 grant from the Ministerio de Ciencia e Innovación. Batory is retired, writing free textbooks [5], and is walking dogs for wages.

References

1. Agh, H., García, F., Piattini, M.: A checklist for the evaluation of software process line approaches. Inf. Softw. Technol. **146**(1) (2022)
2. Apel, S., Batory, D., Kästner, C., Saake, G.: Feature-oriented Software Product Lines. Springer, NY (2016). https://doi.org/10.1007/978-3-642-37521-7
3. Barrett, C.: Decision procedures: an algorithmic point of view, by Daniel Kroening and Ofer Strichman,Springer-Verlag, 2008. J. Autom. Reasoning **51**(4), 453–456 (2013)

4. Barrett, C., Tinelli, C.: Satisfiability Modulo Theories (2018). https://doi.org/10.1007/978-3-319-10575-8_11
5. Batory, D.: Automated Software Design, vol. 1 (2021). Lulu.com
6. Bąk, K., Czarnecki, K., Wąsowski, A.: Feature and meta-models in Clafer: mixed, specialized, and coupled. In: Malloy, B., Staab, S., van den Brand, M. (eds.) SLE 2010. LNCS, vol. 6563, pp. 102–122. Springer, Heidelberg (2011). https://doi.org/10.1007/978-3-642-19440-5_7
7. Benavides, D., Segura, S., Ruiz-Cortés, A.: Automated analysis of feature models 20 years later: a literature review. Inf. Syst. **35**(6), 615–636 (2010)
8. Berger, T., She, S., Lotufo, R., Wąsowski, A., Czarnecki, K.: A study of variability models and languages in the systems software domain. IEEE TSE **39**(12), 1611–1640 (2013)
9. Biere, A., Heule, M., van Maaren, H.: Handbook of Satisfiability. IOS Press, Amsterdam (2009)
10. Brummayer, R., Biere, A.: Boolector: an efficient SMT solver for bit-vectors and arrays. In: Kowalewski, S., Philippou, A. (eds.) TACAS 2009. LNCS, vol. 5505, pp. 174–177. Springer, Heidelberg (2009). https://doi.org/10.1007/978-3-642-00768-2_16
11. Bryant, R.E., Kroening, D., Ouaknine, J., Seshia, S.A., Strichman, O., Brady, B.: Deciding bit-vector arithmetic with abstraction. In: Grumberg, O., Huth, M. (eds.) TACAS 2007. LNCS, vol. 4424, pp. 358–372. Springer, Heidelberg (2007). https://doi.org/10.1007/978-3-540-71209-1_28
12. Bryant, R.E.: Binary decision diagrams. In: Handbook of Model Checking, pp. 191–217. Springer, Cham (2018). https://doi.org/10.1007/978-3-319-10575-8_7
13. Chakraborty, S., et al.: Approximate model counting. FRONTIERS (2021)
14. Chistikov, D., Dimitrova, R., Majumdar, R.: Approximate counting in SMT and value estimation for probabilistic programs. Acta Informatica **54**(8) (2017)
15. Döller, V., Karagiannis, D.: Formalizing conceptual modeling methods with META-MORPH. In: Augusto, A., Gill, A., Nurcan, S., Reinhartz-Berger, I., Schmidt, R., Zdravkovic, J. (eds.) BPMDS/EMMSAD -2021. LNBIP, vol. 421, pp. 245–261. Springer, Cham (2021). https://doi.org/10.1007/978-3-030-79186-5_16
16. Ganesh, V., Dill, D.: The Simple Theorem Prover (STP) solver (2006). https://stp.github.io/
17. Henard, C., Papadakis, M., Harman, M., Traon, Y.L.: Combining multi-objective search and constraint solving for configuring large software product lines. In: SPLC. IEEE Press (2015)
18. Horcas, J., Pinto, M., Fuentes, L.: Variability models for generating efficient configurations of functional quality attributes. IST J. **95** (2018)
19. Horcas, J., Pinto, M., Fuentes, L.: Extensible and modular abstract syntax for feature modeling based on language constructs. In: SPLC. ACM (2020)
20. Kästner, C., et al.: Variability-aware parsing in the presence of lexical macros and conditional compilation. In: OOPSLA, vol. 46. IEEE/ACM (2011)
21. Liang, J., Ganesh, V., Czarnecki, K., Raman, V.: SAT-based analysis of large real-world feature models is easy. In: SPLC. IEEE/ACM (2015)
22. Marchezan, L., Rodrigues, E., Assunção, W.K.G., Bernardino, M., Basso, F.P., Carbonell, J.: Software product line scoping: a systematic literature review. J. Syst. Softw. **186** (2022)
23. de Moura, L., Bjørner, N.: Z3: an efficient SMT solver. In: Ramakrishnan, C.R., Rehof, J. (eds.) TACAS 2008. LNCS, vol. 4963, pp. 337–340. Springer, Heidelberg (2008). https://doi.org/10.1007/978-3-540-78800-3_24

24. Munoz, D.-J., Gurov, D., Pinto, M., Fuentes, L.: Category theory framework for variability models with non-functional requirements. In: La Rosa, M., Sadiq, S., Teniente, E. (eds.) CAiSE 2021. LNCS, vol. 12751, pp. 397–413. Springer, Cham (2021). https://doi.org/10.1007/978-3-030-79382-1_24

25. Munoz, D.J., Pinto, M., Fuentes, L.: Finding correlations of features affecting energy consumption and performance of web servers using the HADAS eco-assistant. Computing **100**(11), 1155–1173 (2018)

26. Munoz, D., Oh, J., Pinto, M., Fuentes, L., Batory, D.: Uniform random sampling product configurations of feature models that have numerical features. In: SPLC (2019)

27. Munoz, D., Pinto, M., Fuentes, L.: HADAS: analysing quality attributes of software configurations. In: SPLC, SPLC 2019. ACM (2019)

28. Oh, J., Batory, D., Myers, M., Siegmund, N.: Finding near-optimal configurations in product lines by random sampling. In: ESEC/FSE (2017)

29. Oh, J., Gazillo, P., Batory, D., Heule, M., Myers, M.: Uniform Sampling from Kconfig Feature Models. Technical report, TR-19-02, University of Texas at Austin, Department of Computer Science (2019)

30. Pett, T., Thüm, T., Runge, T., Krieter, S., Lochau, M., Schaefer, I.: Product sampling for product lines: the scalability challenge. In: SPLC, SPLC 2019. Association for Computing Machinery (2019)

31. Phan, Q.: Model counting modulo theories. Ph.D. thesis, Queen Mary University of London, April 2015

32. Heradio, R., Fernandez-Amoros, D., Galindo, J., Benavides, D., Batory, D.: Uniform and scalable sampling of highly configurable systems. Empir. Softw. Eng. **27**, 44 (2022)

33. Raatikainen, M., Tiihonen, J., Mannisto, T.: Software product lines and variability modeling: a tertiary study. J. Syst. Softw. **149**, 485 510 (2019)

34. Rossi, F., Beek, P.V., Walsh, T.: Handbook of Constraint Programming. Elsevier (2006)

35. Schmitt, A., Wiersch, S., Weis, S.: Glencoe-a Visualization Prototyping Framework. In: ICCE (2015)

36. Shi, K.: Combining evolutionary algorithms with constraint solving for configuration optimization. In: ICSME. IEEE/ACM, September 2017

37. Siegmund, N., Grebhahn, A., Apel, S., Kästner, C.: Performance-influence models for highly configurable systems. In: FSE. ACM, New York (2015)

38. Sorensson, N., Een, N.: Minisat v1. 13-a SAT solver with conflict-clause minimization. SAT **2005**(53), 1–12 (2005)

39. Sundermann, C., Nieke, M., Bittner, P.M., Heß, T., Thüm, T., Schaefer, I.: Applications of #SAT solvers on feature models. In: VaMoS. ACM (2021)

40. Surveysystem.com: Sample Size Calc. https://www.surveysystem.com/sscalc.htm

41. Thüm, T., et al.: FeatureIDE: an extensible framework for feature-oriented software development. Sci. Comput. Program. **79**, 70–85 (2014)

42. Thurley, M.: sharpSAT – counting models with advanced component caching and implicit BCP. In: Biere, A., Gomes, C.P. (eds.) SAT 2006. LNCS, vol. 4121, pp. 424–429. Springer, Heidelberg (2006). https://doi.org/10.1007/11814948_38

43. Tseitin, G.: On the complexity of derivation in propositional calculus. In: Siekmann, J., Wrightson, G. (eds.) Automation of Reasoning: 2: Classical Papers on Computational Logic 1967–1970. Springer, Heidelberg (1983). https://doi.org/10.1007/978-3-642-81955-1_28

Evolution and Reuse

Evolution Support for Custom Variability Artifacts Using Feature Models: A Study in the Cyber-Physical Production Systems Domain

Kevin Feichtinger[1]([✉]) [iD], Kristof Meixner[2,3] [iD], Stefan Biffl[2,4],
and Rick Rabiser[1,5] [iD]

[1] LIT CPS Lab, Johannes Kepler University Linz, Linz, Austria
kevin.feichtinger@jku.at
[2] Institute of Information Systems Engineering, TU Vienna, Vienna, Austria
[3] Christian Doppler Laboratory SQI, TU Vienna, Vienna, Austria
kristof.meixner@tuwien.ac.at
[4] Austrian Competence Center for Digital Production, Vienna, Austria
stefan.biffl@tuwien.ac.at
[5] Christian Doppler Laboratory VaSiCS, Johannes Kepler University Linz,
Linz, Austria
rick.rabiser@jku.at

Abstract. Cyber-Physical Production Systems (CPPSs) are constantly evolving, highly configurable, complex software-intensive systems interacting with their environment. The variability of CPPSs must be well-documented to foster reuse, for which the Software Product Line (SPL) community proposed variability models. Unfortunately, industry is mostly unaware of existing variability modeling approaches and frequently develops custom artifacts to document variability, e.g., spreadsheets or Domain-Specific Languages (DSLs). In contrast to SPL variability models, the evolution of these custom artifacts is hardly researched and evolving them remains a tedious and error-prone manual task in practice. In this paper, using two CPPS case studies, we investigate the impact of system evolution on custom artifacts and feature models as a basis for further research. We discuss how feature models could benefit the evolution of DSL-based variability artifacts.

Keywords: Variability modeling · Variability evolution · Custom variability artifacts · Feature models · Cyber-physical production system

1 Introduction

Cyber-Physical Production Systems (CPPSs) are highly configurable production systems with real-time control and self-adaptive behaviour [11]. A sound

© Springer Nature Switzerland AG 2022
G. Perrouin et al. (Eds.): ICSR 2022, LNCS 13297, pp. 79–84, 2022.
https://doi.org/10.1007/978-3-031-08129-3_5

documentation of their variability is required to foster reuse [3]. For this purpose, the Software Product Line (SPL) community proposed many different variability modeling approaches [12], which are used to explicitly model common and variable characteristics of a set of (software-intensive) systems [1,7]. Unfortunately, industry is mostly unaware of the plethora of existing variability modeling approaches from academia and frequently develops their own custom solutions, e.g., spreadsheet-based representations or Domain-Specific Languages (DSLs) [1]. For instance, in CPPS engineering the DSL-based variability artifact Product-Process-Resource DSL (PPR–DSL) [10] is used.

Frequently changing customer needs and environmental requirements lead to constantly evolving products. Implementation and (variability) documentation must thus be frequently adapted. Without proper tool support, this can be a tedious task in practice [13]. The goal of our research is to *enable industrial practitioners to evolve their custom variability artifacts supported by a variability model.* We do not aim to replace custom variability artifacts used in industry. However, we argue that using a variability model, i.e., a feature model, could benefit the evolution of custom variability artifacts, i.e., PPR–DSL artifacts. This paper investigates the product line evolution impact on PPR–DSL artifacts compared to feature models, using two case study systems from the CPPS domain, which are available as PPR–DSL artifacts and part of the ESPLA catalog [7,9].

2   CPPS Case Studies

We use two case study systems from the CPPS domain: the *Water filter* and *Rocker Switch* from the ESPLA catalog [7,9], which are available as PPR–DSL [10] artifacts. We only provide a brief overview on the case studies here and refer the reader to Meixner et al.'s [9] paper for further details, especially on the PPR–DSL artifacts.

The *Water filter* product line aims to develop a low-cost, customizable water filtering solution, which works without electricity and is easy to manufacture [6]. In its base version, the *Water filter* consists of 8 different filters by combining 26 unique components. Figure 1 shows a FeatureIDE [8] feature model of its base version.

Fig. 1. Feature model of the *Water filter* case study [9].

The *Rocker Switch* case study builds a set of switches, used in a variety of different applications (e.g., electrical devices or lights) [9]. The product line allows to build 16 different switches from 15 components. 13 components are mandatory. Figure 2 shows a FeatureIDE [8] feature model of the product line.

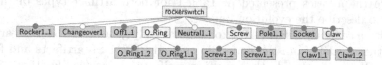

Fig. 2. Feature model of the *Rocker Switch* case study [9].

Table 1. Metrics we collect for PPR–DSL artifacts and feature models.

Type	Metric	Description
PPR–DSL artif.	#P	Number of products
	$\#P_{comp}$	Number of products specifying the attribute component
	$\#P_{abst}$	Number of abstract products
	$\#P_{impl}$	Number of products, which implement at least one other product
	$\#P_{child}$	Number of products, which specify children
	$\#C_{req}$	Number of products, which require at least one other product
	$\#C_{excl}$	Number of products, which exclude at least one other product
	$\#C_{complex}$	Number of constraints including more than two products
Feature Model	#F	Number of features
	$\#F_{abst}$	Number of abstract features
	$\#F_{man}$	Number of mandatory features
	$\#C_{xorgroup}$	Number of Xor group constraints
	$\#C_{total}$	Number of constraints
	$\#C_{complex}$	Number of constraints, which involve more than two features
	Tree height	Feature model tree height
	#Configs	Number of valid configurations found using sampling

3 Method

For our evolution analysis, we define and perform evolution scenarios on two case study systems, i.e., *S1: Add new, optional feature, S2: Add new, dependent feature:, S3: Add multiple features and constraints within product line scope, S4: Add multiple new features and constraints outside the scope, S5:Add constraints and remove features.* We use existing metrics for feature models [2] to assess their general characteristics [4], size and complexity. Building on these metrics, we identified similar metrics to assess these aspects for PPR–DSL artifacts. We assess the evolution impact on the PPR–DSL artifacts and feature models using metric changes after each evolution step. Table 1 summarizes the investigated metrics for PPR–DSL artifacts (upper part) and feature models (lower part). A detailed description of the evolution scenarios and the metrics we used to measure evolution impact can be found in an online appendix to this paper.[1]

Both case studies provide PPR–DSL artifacts, from which we derive feature models to perform our study, using TRAVART [5].[2] Then, we manually conduct the evolution scenarios on each case study's artifacts. Due to missing tool

[1] https://doi.org/10.5281/zenodo.6388741.
[2] https://github.com/tuw-qse/cpps-var-case-studies.

support, we edited the PPR–DSL artifacts manually in a text editor, whereas we used FeatureIDE [8] to edit the feature models. We thereby created two independent evolution histories for each case study, which we provide online.[3] We calculate the metrics presented in Table 1 for both artifact types of the case studies to describe the evolution impact.

We then again use TRAVART to automatically generate PPR–DSL artifacts and feature models from the manually created PPR–DSL artifacts and feature models. We again provide the resulting artifacts online (see Footnote 3). We again collect the proposed metrics for the automatically derived artifacts and discuss the metrics to the manually created ones by computing the delta between the metrics of the transformed artifact minus the same version of the original artifact.

4   Evolution Analysis Results

We present the results of our evolution analysis for both case studies in Table 2. A textual description of the table is available in an online appendix (see Footnote 1) and the created artifacts are available online. (see Footnote 3) Here we only discuss two key takeaways:

Variability Analysis Tools Help to Preserve Consistency and Correctness During Evolution: While performing the evolution scenarios and evolving the PPR–DSL artifacts and feature models, we sometimes introduced contradicting constraints in the PPR–DSL artifacts, causing dead features or invalid configurations in the feature model. Such errors happen easily to (also experienced) modelers, especially, as the complexity of the artifacts increases over time. The FeatureIDE [8] tool helped us resolve these issues and keep the feature model, and hence also the PPR–DSL artifact, consistent and correct. Unfortunately, as of now, there is no such tool support available for the PPR–DSL, which would benefit the evolution of these artifacts. Still, this will remain a challenge for other custom variability artifacts from industry such as spreadsheets and needs more attention of researchers.

Transformation Approaches Allow to Work with More than One Type of Artifact and Related Tool Support During Evolution: Notably, most metrics of the transformed PPR–DSL artifacts and feature models remained equal (i.e., zeros in the respective columns) to the original PPR–DSL artifacts and feature models, respectively. Hence, it is possible to evolve either side without losing much artifact information when transforming them to the other artifact type. This is a key benefit of a transformation approach as one can evolve one type of artifact and automatically generate the other. Nevertheless, more research is needed regarding avoiding information loss while transforming the artifacts and how industry can effectively integrate and adapt such an approach. Currently, feature models can be used very effectively to test changes to the product variability and to detect errors and inconsistencies at an early stage.

---

[3] https://doi.org/10.5281/zenodo.6388657.

Table 2. Evolution impact on the two case study systems and the difference.

Case Study	Artifact creation	Scenario	#P	#P comp	#P abst	#P impl	#P child	#C req	#C excl	#C comp	Scenario	#F	#F abst	#F man	#C xorgroup	#C total	#C comp	Tree height	#Configs
Water filter	manual	dsl-s0	9	26	7	22	1	16	18	2	fm-s0	27	7	14	4	18	2	2	8
		dsl-s1	17	27	7	30	1	24	26	2	fm-s1	28	7	14	4	18	2	2	16
		dsl-s2	17	29	8	32	1	25	28	2	fm-s2	30	8	15	5	21	2	2	16
		dsl-s3	25	33	8	40	2	34	37	2	fm-s3	34	8	18	5	26	2	2	20
		dsl-s4	25	49	10	52	3	36	52	9	fm-s4	50	10	18	8	36	9	3	425
		dsl-s5	25	46	10	49	3	37	48	11	fm-s5	47	10	18	8	37	11	3	165
	automatic	fm-s0	0	0	0	0	0	-2	0	0	dsl-s0	0	0	0	0	0	0	0	0
		fm-s1	0	0	0	0	0	-2	0	0	dsl-s1	0	0	0	0	0	0	0	0
		fm-s2	0	0	0	0	0	-2	0	0	dsl-s2	0	0	0	0	+3	0	0	0
		fm-s3	-4	0	0	-1	-1	-6	-4	0	dsl-s3	0	0	0	0	+3	0	0	0
		fm-s4	+401	0	0	+401	-2	+399	+401	0	dsl-s4	0	0	0	0	+3	0	0	0
		fm-s5	+141	0	0	+141	-2	+139	+141	0	dsl-s5	0	0	0	0	+3	0	0	0
Rocker Switch	manual	dsl-s0	5	15	4	10	0	4	4	0	fm-s0	16	4	14	0	0	0	2	4
		dsl-s1	9	16	4	14	0	8	8	0	fm-s1	17	4	14	0	0	0	2	8
		dsl-s2	6	32	9	27	0	13	5	0	fm-s2	33	9	14	0	8	0	2	273
		dsl-s3	6	35	10	29	0	13	7	1	fm-s3	36	10	14	1	9	1	2	337
		dsl-s4	6	40	12	31	1	14	9	1	fm-s4	41	12	16	2	10	1	3	444
		dsl-s5	6	39	12	30	1	13	12	1	fm-s5	40	12	16	2	17	1	3	428
	automatic	fm-s0	0	0	0	0	0	0	0	0	dsl-s0	0	0	0	0	0	0	0	0
		fm-s1	0	0	0	0	0	0	0	0	dsl-s1	0	0	0	0	0	0	0	0
		fm-s2	+268	0	0	+268	0	+269	+268	0	dsl-s2	0	0	0	0	0	0	0	-3
		fm-s3	+332	0	0	+332	0	+333	+332	0	dsl-s3	0	0	0	0	0	0	0	-3
		fm-s4	+439	0	0	+441	-1	+440	+439	0	dsl-s4	0	0	0	0	0	0	0	-3
		fm-s5	+423	0	0	+426	-1	+424	+424	0	dsl-s5	0	0	0	0	0	0	0	-5

5 Conclusion

We investigated the product line evolution impact on PPR–DSL artifacts vs. feature models to analyze differences and better understand the custom variability artifacts' evolution and how a variability model could benefit this evolution.

In future work, we aim to integrate process and resource variability aspects of the PPR–DSL. Moreover, we want to define and evaluate a generally applicable process to evolve different types of custom variability artifacts relying on different variability models types. The results of this study will guide the development of the process. We envision to support industrial practitioners to experiment with different variability models and facilitate their adoption in industry.

Acknowledgements. The financial support by the Christian Doppler Research Association, the Austrian Federal Ministry for Digital and Economic Affairs and the National Foundation for Research, Technology and Development is gratefully acknowledged. This work has been partially supported and funded by the Austrian Research Promotion Agency (FFG) via "Austrian Competence Center for Digital Production" (CDP) under contract nr. 881843.

References

1. Berger, T., et al.: A survey of variability modeling in industrial practice. In: Proceedings 7th International Workshop on Variability Modelling of Software-intensive Systems, pp. 7–14. ACM (2013)
2. El-Sharkawy, S., Yamagishi-Eichler, N., Schmid, K.: Metrics for analyzing variability and its implementation in software product lines: a systematic literature review. Inf. Softw. Technol. **106**, 1–30 (2019)
3. Fadhlillah, H.S., Feichtinger, K., Sonnleithner, L., Rabiser, R., Zoitl, A.: Towards heterogeneous multi-dimensional variability modeling in cyber-physical production systems. In: Proceedings 25th ACM International Systems and Software Product Line Conference, SPLC 2021, pp. 123–129. ACM (2021)
4. Feichtinger, K., Rabiser, R.: Variability model transformations: towards unifying variability modeling. In: Proceedings 46th Euromicro Conference on Software Engineering and Advanced Applications. IEEE, Portoroz (2020)
5. Feichtinger, K., Stöbich, J., Romano, D., Rabiser, R.: TRAVART: an approach for transforming variability models. In: 15th International Working Conference on Variability Modelling of Software-Intensive Systems. ACM (2021)
6. Kiagho, B., Machunda, R., Hilonga, A., Njau, K.: Performance of water filters towards the removal of selected pollutants in Arusha, Tanzania. Tanzania J. Sci. **42**(1), 134–147 (2016)
7. Martinez, J., Assunção, W.K., Ziadi, T.: ESPLA: a catalog of extractive SPL adoption case studies. In: Proceedings 21st International Systems and Software Product Line Conference, pp. 38–41. ACM (2017)
8. Meinicke, J., Thüm, T., Schröter, R., Benduhn, F., Leich, T., Saake, G.: Overview on FeatureIDE. In: Mastering Software Variability with FeatureIDE, pp. 227–234. Springer, Cham (2017). https://doi.org/10.1007/978-3-319-61443-4_19
9. Meixner, K., Feichtinger, K., Rabiser, R., Biffl, S.: A reusable set of real-world product line case studies for comparing variability models in research and practice. In: Proceedings 25th ACM International Systems and Software Product Line Conference, SPLC 2021, pp. 105–112. ACM (2021)
10. Meixner, K., Rinker, F., Marcher, H., Decker, J., Biffl, S.: A domain-specific language for product-process-resource modeling. In: IEEE International Conference on Emerging Technologies and Factory Automation (ETFA). IEEE (2021)
11. Monostori, L.: Cyber-physical production systems: roots, expectations and R&D challenges. Procedia CIRP **17**, 9–13 (2014)
12. Raatikainen, M., Tiihonen, J., Männistö, T.: Software product lines and variability modeling: a tertiary study. J. Syst. Softw. **149**, 485–510 (2019)
13. Seidl, C., Heidenreich, F., Aßmann, U.: Co-evolution of models and feature mapping in software product lines. In: Proceedings 16th International Software Product Line Conference - Volume 1, SPLC 2012, pp. 76–85. ACM (2012)

Prevalence and Evolution of License Violations in npm and RubyGems Dependency Networks

Ilyas Saïd Makari, Ahmed Zerouali[✉], and Coen De Roover

Software Languages Lab, Vrije Universiteit Brussel, Brussels, Belgium
{ilyas.said.makari,ahmed.zerouali,coen.de.roover}@vub.be

Abstract. It can be challenging to manage an open source package from a licensing perspective. License violations can be introduced by both direct and indirect package dependencies, which evolve independently. In this paper, we propose a license compatibility matrix as the foundation for a tool that can help maintainers assess the compliance of their package with the licenses of its dependencies. Using this tool, we empirically study the evolution, popularity, and compliance with dependency licenses in the npm and RubyGems software package ecosystems. The size of the corresponding dependency networks renders verifying license compliance for indirect dependencies computationally expensive. We found that 7.3% of npm packages and 13.9% of RubyGems have direct or indirect dependencies with incompatible licenses. We also found that GPL dependencies are the major cause for incompatibilities. Our results provide a good understanding of the state of license incompatibilities in software package ecosystems, and suggest that individual ecosystems can differ significantly in this regard.

Keywords: Software license · License compatibility · Package dependency · npm · RubyGems

1 Introduction

Open Source Software (OSS) has become the standard in the software industry, encouraging collaboration and reuse. Much of this Open Source Software is reused by developers incorporating it into their own software as independent building blocks, e.g., packages. As a matter of fact, online package repositories, such as npm for JavaScript and RubyGems for Ruby, provide an enormous amount of free open source software packages. These packages are available for any developer to use in their own software, but in many cases under particular restrictions imposed by the package owners. These restrictions constitute a software license.

Open source packages can be distributed under licenses with varying degrees of freedom, decided on by their owner. The variety among license types complicates using multiple package dependencies in one software system. License restrictions of one package may conflict with the restrictions of another, which

© Springer Nature Switzerland AG 2022
G. Perrouin et al. (Eds.): ICSR 2022, LNCS 13297, pp. 85–100, 2022.
https://doi.org/10.1007/978-3-031-08129-3_6

encumbers ensuring legal compliance of one's own software with the licenses of its dependencies. Moreover, depending on a package that is in violation of a license may lead to one's own software violating the same license.

To make sure no conflicts will occur, developers can review each package's license prior to incorporating it into their own software. However, this quickly becomes cumbersome when these used packages depend on other packages, which may in turn depend on other packages, and so on, forming a huge network of directly and indirectly incorporated dependencies. Worse, developers have no control over the dependencies that get included transitively into their software. Online package repositories such as npm and RubyGems which form massive dependency networks only aggravate the problem.

In this paper, we conduct an empirical study into the prevalence and evolution of open source package licensing. Using a license compatibility matrix that includes more licenses than prior work, we study the severity of license incompatibilities in the dependency networks of npm and RubyGems, while distinguishing between incompatibilities with direct or indirect dependencies. More concretely, we study the following research questions:

RQ_1: **What are the most prevalent licenses in package repositories?**
RQ_2: **To which extent do packages rely on direct dependencies with incompatible licenses?**
RQ_3: **How does license incompatibility spread across package dependency networks?**

The tool used to answer these questions can also be used as support by package maintainers in detecting dependency license incompatibilities for their software.

2   Background and Related Work

This section provides the necessary background information and an overview of the related work concerning the use of licenses and compliance therewith.

2.1   Software Licenses

Under the Berne Convention, the international agreement concerning copyright law, an author automatically obtains the exclusive copyright to their work. This applies to software as well, implying that software creators have the ultimate say when it comes to granting rights and placing restrictions. The latter are typically expressed through a software license, i.e., a contract between the copyright holder (licensor) and the user of the software (licensee). For open source software, it is generally advised to choose from an existing license that has already been reviewed by organizations such as the Open Source Initiative (OSI) and the Free Software Foundation (FSF). The SPDX[1] standard provides a unique agreed-upon identifier for each such license. They can be categorized as follows from least to most restrictive:

---

[1] https://spdx.org/licenses/.

- **Public domain**: Software that is released into the public domain is free to use, copy, modify, distribute and sell without any restrictions or attribution required. For example, the "Unlicense" is a template for dedicating software to the public domain. Note that software with no specific license mentioned cannot be automatically interpreted as public domain[2].
- **Permissive licenses**: Software released under permissive licenses (i.e., MIT and Apache), have little restrictions imposed. Permissive licenses allow software reuse for any purpose, but redistributions and derivatives of the work must include the copyright and license notice from the original author. In general, there are little to no restrictions that will cause conflicts when a permissive license is combined with stricter ones.
- **Copyleft licenses**: These form the most restrictive category of OSS licenses, due to their prohibition of proprietization. They require any derivative work to be distributed under a license that preserves all the rights established by the original license. The most popular example is the GPL license, which, among other restrictions, requires derivatives to be licensed under the same GPL license. Copyleft licenses that impose these rules on any kind of derivative work are called strong copyleft licenses, whereas weak copyleft licenses make exceptions for some types of derivative work. For example, weak copyleft licenses like LGPL make exceptions when the original work is used as an independent building block (e.g., a library). In addition, there are network copyleft licenses that expand strong copyleft licenses to software that can be ran via internet or other networks, e.g., AGPL and OSL 3.0.

2.2 License Compliance

Despite the ubiquity of OSS packages, one must be careful when incorporating them as a software dependency. For example, the licenses of two dependencies may contain contradictory statements, rendering their combination legally impossible. This may also be the case for the license of the software into which the package is included. For instance, software released under the permissive MIT license cannot include packages released under the more restrictive GPL license as GPL requires all derivatives to be released under the same license.

In order to identify license incompatibilities, there must be a reliable source of truth that dictates which pairs of licenses are compatible with each other. The FSF provides two lists[3] stating which licenses are (in)compatible with the GPL. However, these lists only provide an answer for a limited number of license combinations. They provide no information about, for instance, the combination of MIT and BSD. Unfortunately, the required source of truth cannot be generated automatically, since licenses are written in natural language with complex legal terms [1]. The following approaches to determining license compatibility have been proposed instead:

---

[2] https://choosealicense.com/no-permission/.
[3] https://www.gnu.org/licenses/license-list.en.html.

- **Set-based approach**: This approach is used by libraries.io's license compatibility tool[4]. Licenses are grouped into disjunct sets ordered from least to most restrictive: public domain, permissive, weak copyleft, strong copyleft, etc. To say that license A is compatible with license B: (1) A must be either public domain, permissive or weak copyleft; or (2) If A is strong copyleft, then B must be either weak copyleft, strong copyleft or network copyleft; or (3) If A is network copyleft, then B must also be network copyleft. However, generalizing license compatibility in this manner will not account for the many exceptions that exist.
- **Formal approach**: This approach was described by Gangadharan et al. [2]. All terms and conditions of licenses are formally specified thus enabling the algorithmic detection of incompatibilities. The algorithm uses the following rule: license A is compatible with license B if all license clauses from A are compatible with those of B. However, it is far from trivial to convert all license text into a formal specification.
- **Graph-based approach**: Relations between different licenses can be modelled using a directed graph [3] in which each node denotes a license and each directed edge between two nodes is used to denote a one-way compatibility, i.e., an edge from license A to license B implies that A is compatible with B, but not necessarily the inverse. Similarly, all licenses that can be reached from license A are also compatible with A. The graph was constructed using the rules that apply when the derivative work is based on the original work. This is important, since weak-copyleft licenses (e.g., LGPL) can make the distinction between work that is "based on a library" and work that "uses a library". Later on, this graph was expanded by Kapitsaki et al. [4] to include additional licenses (e.g., MPL). The resulting graph has subsequently been simplified by removing the incompatibility edges [1].

2.3   Studies on License Compliance in Dependency Networks

Dependency networks are created when one software package depends on other packages which in turn depend on their own packages. The resulting network may aggravate problems detected in a single package, as the issue may rapidly spread to all direct and indirect dependents. This has promoted researchers to conduct studies on license compliance in dependency networks. Kechagia et al. [5] have studied the FreeBSD ports collection from this perspective. They found that GPL-licensed applications that run under FreeBSD use LGPL-licensed components. Qiu et al. [6] have studied the prevalence of dependency-related license violations among 419,708 npm packages. They found that very few packages (0.644%) have dependency-related license violations. In this paper, we found that this proportion increases to 7.3% when we study the entire ecosystem of npm packages while inspecting more license combinations that were not considered in previous studies. In addition, developer surveys in [6] revealed two main

---

[4] https://github.com/librariesio/license-compatibility.

causes for these violations: 1) developers overlook and misunderstand them; and 2) developers find it difficult to manage them and ask for tool support.

Novelty of Our Contribution. Our work extends and updates the insights from previous studies by considering a larger license compatibility matrix that includes additional license combinations. We also carry out an empirical analysis of license violations in both npm and RubyGems dependency networks, and compare them. To the best of our knowledge, we are the first to study licensing in the RubyGems ecosystem. Moreover, we provide a visual tool that helps developers find incompatible transitive dependencies easily.

3 Research Method

This section discusses the details of the research method we used to answer the research questions enumerated in Sect. 1, including how we created an extended license compatibility matrix.

License Compatibility Matrix. We created an extensive and up-to-date compatibility matrix starting from the aforementioned graph proposed by Kapitsaki et al. [1]. The graph alone does not suffice for our study, as it does not include some of the licenses used by popular npm and RubyGems software packages. Moreover, for the context of this work, the meaning of the edges in the graph needs to change from a project being "based on" another project to a project "depending on a library". For example, a project with a permissive license such as MIT is allowed to include an LGPL dependency. This requires including additional edges that account for this possibility. Finally, the absence of a path between two licenses A and B in the graph does not suffice to deem A and B as incompatible. It merely means that the compatibility cannot be determined from the graph alone.

Our matrix therefore aims to provide a definitive answer for as many actual license combinations as possible. To this end, we started from the graph and manually included information from the following sources: (1) the FSF has two lists[5] stating which licenses are compatible and incompatible with the various GPL licenses; (2) the European Commission maintains a matrix that has an answer for a couple more license combinations[6]; and (3) the FSF provides a matrix[7] to determine which (L)GPL licenses are compatible with each other.

Currently, our license compatibility matrix includes 1,681 pairs of licenses. However, it does mark the compatibility of 205 (12.2%) license pairs as "Unknown". These are the license pairs for which we could not determine the compatibility either due to a lack of publicly available information or due to varying opinions among lawyers. Many licenses and combinations thereof remain to be tested in the courts.

---

[5] https://www.gnu.org/licenses/license-list.en.html.

[6] https://ec.europa.eu/jrc/sites/default/files/20150930-second-best-practices-tto-circle-gentile_en.pdf.

[7] https://www.gnu.org/licenses/gpl-faq.en.html.

Package License Extraction: Package managers have a structured method to keep track of metadata, such as licenses and dependencies. Packages from npm come with an automatically created "package.json" manifest that includes these metadata, while RubyGems has "Gemfile". To have the information about licenses used by npm and RubyGems packages, we relied on the latest version of libraries.io Open Data[8] that was released on 12 January 2020. libraries.io dataset contains metadata of packages hosted on 32 different package repositories, including npm and RubyGems. It identifies the licenses of each package using the standardized SPDX identifiers. To identify the versions of the dependencies of each package, we relied on the dependency constraint resolver proposed in [7], which supports the npm and RubyGems package distributions. We determined the appropriate versions of packages to be included for each dependent according to the constraints for its run-time dependencies. As some constraints may resolve to different versions at different points in time, we used the libraries.io snapshot date as the resolution date. This implies that we study licenses in packages as if they were installed or deployed on January 12th, 2020. Having determined the versions of all direct dependencies, we then identify the indirect ones.

More specifically, we inspected $749, 823$ and $94, 953$ npm and RubyGems packages (i.e., their latest version) which depend on $66, 404, 594$ and $1, 190, 422$ run-time dependencies, from which $3, 527, 000$ and $211, 336$ are direct, respectively. We only focused on run-time dependencies because development ones are only needed during development (e.g., unit tests libraries, transpilers, etc.). To determine the license compatibility between a dependency and its dependent, we relied on our license compatibility matrix. A dependency is either compatible, incompatible or unknown. We found that 7.3% (54,778) and 13.9% (13,271) of npm and RubyGems packages have direct or indirect dependencies with incompatible licenses, respectively. We also found the amount of unknown incompatibilities for all (transitive) dependencies to be very small, i.e., 2.9% for npm and 5.6% for RubyGems. After having a deeper look at which license combinations were unknown, it became clear that it mostly consists of multi-licenses, i.e., a package can be used with license A or with license B, e.g., *keypair*[9]. This is due to the fact that our compatibility matrix can only provide answers for pairs of singular licenses. Moreover, there are some packages that can be used with different licenses depending on the third-party that is going to use them. For example, developers of *webgazer*[10] state that their package is *"licensed under GPLv3"* while *"companies have the option to license WebGazer.js under LGPLv3 while their valuation is under $1, 000, 000"*. Extracting such information requires us to process natural language text written in different files like README and then check conditions with dependent packages, which is a complex task. Thus, it is important to note that any incompatibilities with multi-licensed packages will not be taken into account in this study.

---

[8] https://libraries.io/data.

[9] https://www.npmjs.com/package/keypair.

[10] https://www.npmjs.com/package/webgazer.

4   Results

We now evaluate the state of license compliance among the dependency networks formed by the popular package repositories npm and RubyGems.

RQ_1: **What are the Most Prevalent Licenses in Package Repositories?**
We start by determining the most common open source licenses found in each package repository. The ecosystems around some repositories might have a more permissive climate than those around others. According to a blog post [8] from WhiteSource, in 2012 open source software was predominantly using copyleft licenses (59%). Three years later, GitHub [9] reported a shift towards more permissive licenses. With this research question, we want to investigate whether such a shift has also happened among the npm and RubyGems packages, by investigating the evolution of the most popular licenses over time.

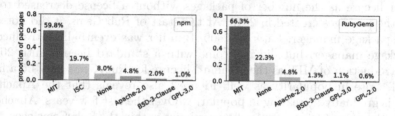

Fig. 1. Top 6 most used licenses

Figure 1 shows the top-6 most popular licenses in npm and RubyGems. We observe that the MIT license is the most popular by far. 59.8% and 66.3% of npm and RubyGems packages make use of the MIT license. Most licenses in the top 6 list are permissive.

From the figure, we also observe that there is a considerable proportion of packages that do not have any license (i.e., *None*), not even a public domain waiver like "Unlicense". This is worrying as without a specified license, no one can copy, distribute, or modify the package except for the original developers. In fact, it is advised not to make use of such software[11]. We expect these packages to cause many license incompatibility problems in package dependency networks.

Figure 2 depicts the evolution of license usage in the npm ecosystem. The X-axis shows the creation date for each package. We observe that the permissive MIT license has been popular since the beginning. Furthermore, in 2014, there seems to be a sudden increase of the ISC license, taking over the popularity of the BSD-3-Clause license. This can be explained by the v1.4.8 update[12] of npm in May 2014, where the previous default license, BSD-3-Clause, was replaced by the ISC license, which is similar to the BSD-2-Clause and MIT licenses. This caused all new npm packages, from May 2014 onwards, to be licensed under the ISC

---

[11] https://choosealicense.com/no-permission/.
[12] https://github.com/npm/cli/blob/latest/changelogs/CHANGELOG-1.md.

license by default. The main difference between ISC and its predecessor is that ISC does not include a non-endorsement statement preventing users of a package to claim they are endorsed by the author of that package. The urge to replace BSD-3-Clause with ISC, might be due to the endorsement of the OpenBSD project [10]. However, in 2015, the Internet Systems Consortium (creators of the ISC license) stated that there is no longer a good reason for ISC to have its own license. Even though ISC is equivalent to the very permissive MIT license, lawyers prefer the more popular license that they are already familiar with [11]. There is now an ongoing discussion in npm to change the default license from ISC to MIT. This is mainly to avoid license proliferation, as the permissive ISC license poses no threats when it comes to license compliance.

Figure 3 shows the evolution of license usage in the RubyGems ecosystem. RubyGems is a repository that has been around for a bit longer, compared to npm. From the figures, we observe that MIT gradually evolved into the most popular license as the number of packages without a license decreased to just 6% of the packages created in 2019. At the start of RubyGems, it did not come with a package manager. Later in 2009, Bundler was eventually introduced as its package manager, but did not come with a standard license until 2011[13]. The introduction of MIT as the standard license for RubyGems may be a factor to MIT's rise in popularity as well. Figure 3 also reveals that the Apache-2.0 license is gradually increasing in popularity. Over the last few years, Apache has become the second most popular license choice within the RubyGems ecosystem. Overall, the climate of the ecosystem is predominantly permissive. However, even though Apache-2.0 is a permissive license, it is not fully compatible with the GPL. Apache-2.0 is only compatible with GPLv3. Thus, developers have to be careful not to use any Apache-licensed dependencies in their GPLv2-licensed software directly or indirectly.

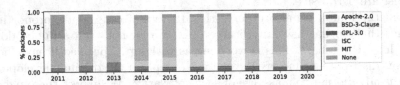

Fig. 2. Proportion of npm packages grouped by license and year of release.

---

[13] https://github.com/rubygems/bundler/blob/master/CHANGELOG.md.

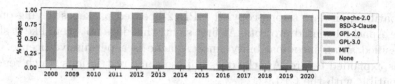

Fig. 3. Proportion of RubyGems packages grouped by license and year of release.

RQ_2: To which Extent do Packages Rely on Direct Dependencies with Incompatible Licenses?

Developers have full control over which direct dependencies to incorporate. Thus, it should be easier for them to verify compliance with direct dependencies, compared to transitive dependencies. However, developers often have to rely on their own knowledge of legal compliance when declaring a license for their own software, allowing room for mistakes. Although tools exist to detect license incompatibilities, they are far from perfect. With RQ_2, we aim to answer to which extent incompatibilities are caused by direct dependencies.

After computing all $(dependent, dependency)$ license pairs, we found that the proportion of direct dependencies with incompatible licenses is low. We only found 32,323 (0.89%) and 11,121 (4.3%) npm and RubyGems dependencies to have licenses that are incompatible with those of their dependents. These incompatibilities are caused by 11,858 and 3,677 unique npm and RubyGems packages used as dependencies and are affecting 23,178 (3.1%) and 9,387 (9.9%) unique npm and RubyGems dependent packages. One could hypothesize that larger ecosystems with lots of dependencies have a higher chance of containing incompatibilities. Interestingly, the smaller ecosystem (RubyGems) seems to have a higher proportion of incompatible dependencies. A possible explanation for this phenomenon is that developers in large ecosystems may have more choices between packages with equivalent functionalities. This allows them to pick a dependency that fits their licensing needs.

Figure 4 shows the most common incompatible direct *(dependent, dependency)* license pairs for npm and RubyGems packages (Y-axis in log scale). As expected, most of the incompatibilities (i.e., 85% for npm and 76.7% for RubyGems) happen because of the fact that many packages used as dependencies do not have a license, i.e., (_, None) while "_" refers to any license. For dependencies that have a license, we observe that the most common pair of incompatible licenses in npm is (MIT, GPL-3.0), i.e., when permissive MIT packages depend on strong-copyleft GPL packages. This is the epitome of a severe license violation. Beyond unfamiliarity with software licensing, there is no other conceivable reason for developers to incorporate these strong-copyleft-licensed packages directly into their permissive-licensed packages. Interestingly, after a manual inspection of the MIT packages with dependency license incompatibilities, we found that many of the maintainers (especially of the most popular packages) have decided to get rid of their GPL dependencies in the meantime. The second most common incompatible pairs are strong-copyleft GPLv2-licensed packages relying on permissive Apache-licensed projects. At first sight, this does not seem like it should be classified as an incompatibility since Apache is a permissive license. However, as explained before, Apache does impose some restrictions which render it incompatible with the GPLv2.

For RubyGems, we observe one incompatible pair of licenses (MIT, GPL-2.0) that heavily stands out from the other pairs. Again, unfamiliarity with software licensing is a plausible cause. However, the problem gets amplified because RubyGems has proportionally more GPLv2 packages than npm. Additionally, RubyGems is the smaller ecosystem, implying that developers might not always find a permissive-licensed alternative for their GPL-licensed dependency. With deeper inspection, we also noticed that some packages could also benefit from downgrading their license from GPLv3 to GPLv2. This is the case for GPLv3 packages that use GPLv2 dependencies, which is not allowed, but easily be remedied with a downgrade to either GPL-2.0 or GPL-2.0-or-later.

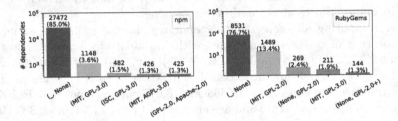

Fig. 4. Top 5 illegal license pairs (dependent, dependency).

RQ_3: How does License Incompatibility Spread Across Package Dependency Networks?

The previous research question focused solely on the direct dependencies, i.e., the dependencies over which the maintainer of a project has complete control. As mentioned before, the maintainer does not have control over which indirect dependencies are used by their project's (in)direct dependencies. Thus, it becomes harder to verify each of the transitive dependencies for potential license incompatibilities. This research question therefore aims to answer to which extent incompatibilities are caused by transitive dependencies. To this end, we will evaluate how prevalent incompatibilities are at each level in the dependency tree of a package. This provides insights into the difficulties maintainers face in keeping track of their transitive dependencies, and into the propagation of incompatibilities through the dependency networks formed by package repositories such as npm and RubyGems.

We start by comparing the proportions of incompatible license pairs between these repositories. We found that npm packages have more indirect dependencies with incompatible licenses than RubyGems. This is due to the high number of dependencies that npm packages include. The latter have license incompatibility with 58,388 indirect dependencies, while RubyGems packages have 8,562.

However, RubyGems has proportionally more incompatible indirect dependencies than npm (i.e., 0.82% against 0.09%, respectively).

Figure 5 depicts the proportion of license incompatibilities at each level in the packages' dependency trees, including the first level (i.e., direct dependencies). We notice that for both package repositories, the proportion of incompatible dependencies decreases from one level to the next until the deepest levels where we see a rise again. The latter is more outspoken for RubyGems, where the proportion of incompatible dependencies is higher than 5% at the 8th and 9th levels. A closer inspection revealed that this is mainly because of the set of *metanorma-x* packages (e.g., *metanorma-gb and metanorma-vsd*) which have a BSD-2-Clause license but indirectly depend on the package *latex-decode* which has a GPL-3.0 license. Note that with these two licenses, it is legal to have a license pair (GPL-3.0, BSD-2-Clause), but not the other way around (BSD-2-Clause, GPL-3.0). Finally, we found that dependencies without a license constitute 86% of license incompatibilities with indirect dependencies for both package repositories.

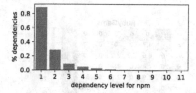 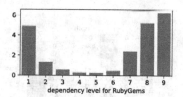

Fig. 5. The proportion of incompatibilities in each level in the dependency tree.

Figure 6 shows the most common illegal pairs of licenses of the format (*dependent, indirect dependency*) that were found at each level of the packages' dependency trees. We observe that the number of dependencies without a license decreases from one level to the next as we go deeper in both package repositories. This means that packages that can be found at deeper levels of the dependency tree usually have a license. One reason might be that deeper packages provide core functionalities and are thus more popular with a more mature management of legal issues such as licensing. We also observe that (MIT, GPL) is less common in indirect dependencies, compared to direct dependencies (See RQ_2). In fact, this is more relevant in the case of npm where we see that (GPL-2.0, Apache-2.0) is the most common incompatible license pair. Interestingly, the number of (MIT, GPL) pairs seems to gradually decrease from a dependency tree level to another while the second-most common illegal pair increases: (GPL-2.0, Apache-2.0). This means that the Apache-2.0 license is more common among the deeper levels. Consequently, direct incompatibilities with this Apache license are more likely in deeper levels.

One hypothesis explaining this phenomenon is that some core packages make use of the Apache-2.0 license. These would be packages that are important but are not regularly needed as direct dependencies, which is why they occur more as indirect dependencies. Such packages are more likely to be older packages which happened to be licensed under Apache 2.0 before the dominance increase of MIT and ISC licenses.

Having a closer look at the concrete packages that reside in the deeper levels, we indeed found that these are packages that provide core functionalities. Examples of these Apache-licensed packages at the deeper levels are *thread_safe* and *addressable* from RubyGems, and *oauth-sign, forever-agent, aws-sign2* and *caseless* from npm. These are popular packages downloaded millions of times and they were all released years ago. Moreover, some of them have not been updated for more than three years. In fact we noticed that most Apache-licensed packages that occur at the deeper levels in npm happen to be coming from the same organization. This is an interesting observation as it shows the influence that one single organization can have in a software ecosystem. By choosing the Apache license for all their packages that provide core functionalities, they unwillingly prevent other developers from releasing their software under the GPLv2. However, several package developers are unaware of this incompatibility or simply do not care, making (GPL, Apache) the most common illegal license pair.

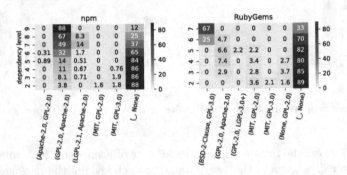

Fig. 6. Top illegal license pairs (dependent, indirect dependency) and their proportion in each level in the dependency tree.

5   Discussion

In RQ_1 we found that package repositories have indeed moved towards a more permissive climate. The MIT license, with its permissive and simple nature, has become the primary license of choice for many open source developers both in npm and RubyGems. An important factor that limits the license choice are the chosen third-party dependencies. If one must comply with the licenses of every used dependency, the options become limited, especially when strong-copyleft licensed dependencies are being used. Furthermore, ecosystems that predominantly contain copyleft packages, cause all other packages that depend on them to also be copyleft. *WordPress* plugins[14] form a good example of an ecosystem

---

[14] https://choosealicense.com/community/.

in which copyleft licenses are popular. In contrast, we noticed that npm has few copyleft projects, possibly due to the high community appeal for npm packages and JavaScript libraries in general. This is also one of the observations already made in the FreeBSD ecosystem [5].

While having a look at the ecosystems separately in RQ_2, it became clear that both ecosystems are facing the same problems to some extent. The main problem is that some developers directly incorporate dependencies with strong-copyleft licenses or without any license into their permissive-licensed packages. This can be resolved by creating more awareness around this topic within the ecosystem that has formed around the package repositories. We did find, however, that in the meantime some developers had realized their mistakes and got rid of their GPL dependencies. However, the overall prevalence of license dependency incompatibility in package repositories can be easily reduced if packages without a license included one. We would recommend developers of such packages to choose a permissive license such as MIT and ISC, as most of the packages make use of permissive licenses. Another common incompatibility that occurs in both ecosystems is GPLv2 packages using Apache-licensed dependencies. This could be easily solved by upgrading the license from GPL-2.0 to GPL-3.0. One of the main issues that the GPLv3 tried to address was the compatibility with licenses such as Apache.

Given the complexity of assessing license compliance across all dependency tree levels, we hypothesized that most incompatibilities would be caused by licenses of indirect dependencies. After investigating this in RQ_3, we observed the exact opposite happening: the first levels cause many more incompatibilities than the deeper ones, and this in both package repositories. Thus, in general the hypothesis cannot be accepted, although there were some cases where one type of incompatibility was more prominent at deeper levels than at the first levels (e.g., (BSD, GPL) in RubyGems). However, these observations seem to be tied to the practices within the ecosystem and its history rather than a mere consequence of their contributors' unfamiliarity with licensing. For example, we have seen that npm has a high concentration of Apache packages at the deeper levels. Similarly, it was mentioned how all ecosystems have a higher concentration of GPL packages at the first levels than at the deeper levels. Due to the viral nature of the GPL license, the concentration of GPL violations is a higher at the first levels than at the deeper ones.

Our findings have only shed a quantitative light on the prevalence and evolution of license incompatibilities across a package's dependency tree. Further research is needed to understand how developers perceive and resolve these issues in practice, as well as the kind of tool support they require.

Tooling: In order to support software developers, we developed a license compatibility tool that enables developers to cope with different license compatibility issues in their own software distributions. For npm packages, our tool uses a visual representation of a project's dependency tree to easily spot legal issues throughout the different levels of the dependency graph. Our tool is based on a

GitHub project *anvaka/npmgraph.an*[15] that constructs a dependency graph for any given npm package using npm's API. Currently, our tool is limited to npm packages only but we are planning to extend it in the future to support other package repositories as well.

Using our tool[16], maintainers of npm packages can spot possible incompatibilities across all levels of their dependency graph. After activating the license incompatibility tester, the tool will highlight nodes and edges where severe incompatibility is identified with a red color (See Fig. 7).

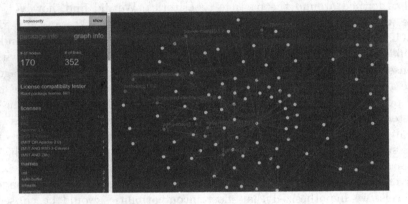

Fig. 7. Screenshot of the license compatibility checking tool.

6   Threats to Validity

The main threat to *construct validity* comes from imprecision in or incompleteness of the data sources we used to identify licenses. We assumed that the libraries.io dataset represents a sound and complete list of packages and their dependencies and licenses. In constructing our license compatibility matrix, we consulted various sources of information. Mistakes in these sources or our interpretation thereof might lead to false positives and false negatives in the compatibility of a license pair. Nevertheless, to mitigate these issues we have conducted manual inspections of samples of the data to verify their soundness.

As a threat to *conclusion validity*, to identify the license for a package, we only considered the license of the latest release of each package. It could be possible that some packages have changed their licenses before. However, previous studies have shown that software projects do not usually change their licenses and when they do, they usually migrate to less restrictive licenses [12]. The latter finding means that only considering the license of the latest package releases may lead to

---

[15] https://github.com/anvaka/npmgraph.an.
[16] https://doi.org/10.5281/zenodo.5913761.

an underestimation of the severity of license violations in dependency networks, since older releases of used packages are linked to more restrictive licenses.

Another threat to *conclusion validity* stems from the fact that whenever faced with uncertainty on the compatibility of a license pair, it was marked as "Unknown". Thus, only the most severe incompatibilities were marked as incompatible. Moreover, we only studied packages with a single license. However, we found that the proportion of packages with multiple licenses is small leading to a small proportion of dependencies without a compatibility status "Unknown".

We have also found many packages without a license, which led us to mark any license pair with the format ($_$, *None*) as incompatible[17]. It could be possible that some of these packages without a license intentionally neglected to include a license, which means that our results here represent an overestimation with respect to license incompatibility with dependencies without a license.

7 Conclusion

This study evaluated the severity of license violations across transitive dependencies of npm and RubyGems packages. We hypothesized that due to the complexity of manually assessing compliance across all levels of a dependency tree, there would be more incompatibilities caused by deeper-level dependencies. Contrary to the hypothesis, this study has shown that deeper-level dependencies cause fewer incompatibilities than those at the shallow levels. Besides dependencies without a license, we found that GPL dependencies are the major cause for incompatibilities, and that they are more present in the first level of dependency trees. Furthermore, this study has also shown how a set of packages created by a single organization can influence an ecosystem when it consistently releases useful packages under a particular license. For future work, we plan to investigate the impact of the license preferences of an individual or organisation in OSS package repositories even further. Finally, to assist developers in detecting and resolving these issues, we have created a graphical tool out of the algorithm at the heart of our empirical study.

Acknowledgments. This research was partially funded by the Excellence of Science project 30446992 SECO-Assist financed by F.R.S.-FNRS and FWO-Vlaanderen.

References

1. Kapitsaki, G.M., Kramer, F., Tselikas, N.D.: Automating the license compatibility process in open source software with SPDX. J. Syst. Softw. **131**, 386–401 (2017)
2. Gangadharan, G.R., D'Andrea, V., De Paoli, S., Weiss, M.: Managing license compliance in free and open source software development. Inf. Syst. Front. **14**(2), 143–154 (2012)

---

[17] In ($_$, *None*), "$_$" refers to dependent with any license and *None* refers to dependency without a license.

3. Wheeler, D.A.: The free-libre/open source software (floss) license slide, September 2007
4. Kapitsaki, G.M., Tselikas, N.D., Foukarakis, I.E.: An insight into license tools for open source software systems. J. Syst. Softw. **102**, 72–87 (2015)
5. Kechagia, M., Spinellis, D., Androutsellis-Theotokis, S.: Open source licensing across package dependencies. In: 2010 14th Panhellenic Conference on Informatics, pp. 27–32. IEEE (2010)
6. Qiu, S., German, D.M., Inoue, K.: Empirical study on dependency-related license violation in the javascript package ecosystem. J. Inf. Process. **29**, 296–304 (2021)
7. Decan, A., Mens, T.: What do package dependencies tell us about semantic versioning? IEEE Trans. Softw. Eng. **47**(6), 1226–1240 (2019)
8. Michaeli, S.: Top 10 open source software licenses of 2016 and key trends. https://resources.whitesourcesoftware.com/blog-whitesource/top-10-open-source-software-licenses-of-2016-and-key-trends. January 2017
9. Balter, B.: Open source license usage on github.com. https://github.blog/2015-03-09-open-source-license-usage-on-github-com/. March 2015
10. Openbsd Copyright Policy. https://www.openbsd.org/policy.html
11. Reid, B.: Kea to be released under mozilla public license 2.0, December 2015
12. Vendome, C., Linares-Vásquez, M., Bavota, G., Di Penta, M., German, D., Poshyvanyk, D.: License usage and changes: a large-scale study of java projects on github. In: 2015 IEEE 23rd International Conference on Program Comprehension, pp. 218–228. IEEE (2015)

Quality, Longevity and Reuse

Differential Testing of Simulation-Based Virtual Machine Generators
Automatic Detection of VM Generator Semantic Gaps Between Simulation and Generated VMs

Pierre Misse-chanabier[1(✉)], Guillermo Polito[2(✉)], Noury Bouraqadi[3(✉)],

Stéphane Ducasse[1(✉)], Luc Fabresse[3(✉)], and Pablo Tesone[2(✉)]

[1] Inria, Univ Lille, CNRS, Centrale Lille, UMR 9189 - CRIStAL, Lille 59000, France
{Pierre.Misse-Chanabier,Stephane.Ducasse}@inria.fr
[2] CNRS, UMR 9189 - CRIStAL, Univ Lille, Centrale Lille, Inria, Lille 59000, France
{Guillermo.Polito,Pablo.Tesone}@inria.fr
[3] IMT Nord Europe, Institut Mines-Télécom, Univ. Lille, Centre for Digital Systems,
Douai 59500, France
{Noury.Bouraqadi,Luc.Fabresse}@imt-nord-europe.fr

Abstract. Testing and debugging language Virtual Machines (VMs) is a laborious task without the proper tooling. This complexity is aggravated when the VM targets multiple architectures. To solve this problem, simulation-based VM generator frameworks allow one to write test cases on the simulation, but those test cases do not ensure the correctness of the generated artifact due to the semantic gaps between the simulated VM and generated VMs.

We propose Test Transmutation to extend simulation-based VM generator frameworks to support test case generation. It validates the generated VM by also running test cases generated from existing simulation test cases. Results of the generated test cases are compared against the simulation test cases using differential testing. Moreover, test cases are automatically mutated with non-semantic-preserving mutations.

Test Transmutation detects bugs that are representative of typical VM modifications. We demonstrate its effectiveness by applying it to a set of real test cases of the Pharo VM. It allowed us to find several issues that were unknown to the VM development team. Our approach shows promising results to test simulation-based VM generator frameworks.

Keywords: Testing · Virtual Machine · Code mutation · Simulation

1 Introduction

Modern language implementations are based on language Virtual Machines (VMs) enabling features such as automatic memory management and JIT compilation. To cope with the elevated cost of building language VMs, there are three main kinds of solutions. First, *VM generation frameworks* help with interpreter generation and JIT compiler generation [9,13,15,18,25,31,40]. Second, *Metacircular VMs* such as Maxine [39], Self [38] and Squawk [34] provide rich VMs development environments that allow live

G. Perrouin et al. (Eds.): ICSR 2022, LNCS 13297, pp. 103–119, 2022.
https://doi.org/10.1007/978-3-031-08129-3_7

debugging. Third, *simulation-based VM generators* are VM generation frameworks with simulation environments easing VM development and debugging. Examples of this last approach are the OpenSmalltalk-VM for Pharo and Squeak [18,25], and PyPy VM[1] which is supported by the RPython framework [31]. A main challenge of using such simulation-based VM generator frameworks is the *semantic gaps* [6] between the simulated VM and the generated VMs. Semantic gaps are differences in the semantic before and after compilation. Examples of the semantic gaps are differences in typing or abstraction level, which make simulation environments not functionally equivalent to the generation target environments [29].

Testing and debugging VMs is a laborious task without the proper tooling, which is aggravated when the VM targets multiple architectures [5]. Simulation-based VM environments allow one to write test cases on the simulation environment, but those test cases do not ensure the correctness of the generated VM. Recently, the team of Maxine and Pharo reported QEMU-based[2] test infrastructures for testing and debugging [20, 30]. Maxine's Metacircular approach compiles directly to machine code, losing its rich debugging capabilities when bootstrapping in a new platform. Pharo's approach benefits from the simulation, but tests only the simulated VM. Finally, an abundance of work exists on compiler testing outside of the VM community [10], but these works are not directly applicable to the VM field.

In this article, we propose a novel approach to test simulation-based VM generator frameworks that we call Test Transmutation. We propose to extend such frameworks to also reuse simulation test cases. We generate the test cases along with the VM and execute them on the generated VM. We use differential testing [23] to compare the generated test results against the simulation test results for each test case. Moreover, generated test cases are also impacted by semantic gaps such as the typing differences. To minimize the test cases' semantic gaps, we mutate the test cases [19]. Test cases with different test results, mutated or not, are evidence of bugs in the VM or VM generator.

We validate that our approach detects errors by manually introducing bugs in the Pharo VM code. We perform an empirical analysis applying our approach to a subset of the Pharo VM test cases. Although this VM has been stable and industrially-used for decades, we find bugs on the VM generation and simulation. Our analysis shows that our approach is promising to test simulation-based VM generator frameworks.

The contributions of this paper are the following:

– A testing approach for simulation-based VM generators.
– Validation of a code generation framework using *non-semantic-preserving muta-tions* together with differential testing.

To the best of our knowledge, we are the first to propose such an approach to validate a code generation framework.

We first explain why testing only the simulation in simulation-based VM generator frameworks is insufficient (Sect. 2). We then present Test Transmutation (Sect. 3) and our experimental context (Sect. 4). We validate that Test Transmutation detects manually introduced bugs (Sect. 5). We also show empirical evidence of Test Transmutation

---

[1] www.pypy.org.
[2] https://www.qemu.org.

on an industry level VM (Sect. 6). Finally, we present the relevant related work (Sect. 7) before concluding the paper (Sect. 8).

2   Problem: Testing Simulation-Based VM Generators Frameworks

Simulation-based VM generator frameworks propose two modes of execution: the simulated execution and the generated code execution. Most debugging and development happens in the simulation environment, and once the VM is ready, it is compiled to a machine executable VM [25,31]. However, the simulated VM presents **semantic gaps** [6] with the generated VMs because they trade-off precision for other software qualities such as fast feedback loops. Moreover the test cases are only executed on the simulation environment, but those test cases do not ensure the correctness of the generated VM. This Section presents the semantic gaps problem of simulation-based VM generators and the limits of simulation-based testing with Slang VM generator examples, the simulation-based VM generator framework used by Pharo.

2.1   Example Context: The Slang VM Generator

Pharo is an object-oriented dynamically-typed language from the Smalltalk tradition [7]. The Pharo VM is an industrial level VM written in Pharo itself and generating a C VM using a VM-specific generator called Slang VM generator [18]. The VM implements at the core of its execution engine a threaded bytecode interpreter, a linear non-optimising JIT compiler named Cogit [24] that includes polymorphic inline caches [17] and a generational scavenger garbage collector that uses a copy collector for young objects and a mark-compact collector for older objects [37]. The VM generator is in charge of generating from high-level object-oriented Pharo code, low-level functional/imperative C code and applying VM specific optimizations to it.

2.2   Pharo VM Semantic Gaps by Example

The Slang VM generator takes as input a VM definition written in Pharo itself and generates C code [26]. Code generation does not happen without loss: the Slang VM generator generates an efficient VM by restricting the input language and its generation. Pharo's object-oriented features are either mapped to C code [36] or rejected.

```
1  primitiveNaturalLogarithm
2     <var: receiver type: #double>
3     | receiver |
4     receiver := self stackFloatValue: 0.
5     self successful ifFalse: [ ↑ self primitiveFail ].
6     self putOnStackTopFloatObjectOf:
7         (self generationEnvironment: [ receiver log ]
8             simulationEnvironment: [ receiver ln ])
```

Listing 1.1. Excerpt of VM code for the primitiveNaturalLogarithm. It is showing environment specific code and type annotations that are ignored during simulation.

Let us consider the example in Listing 1.1 that presents some of Slang VM generator features. The example defines a native function (*i.e.,* primitives in Pharo's terminology) computing the natural logarithm from a positive floating point number. The Slang VM generator provides a framework to define stack-based bytecode machines and access the execution stack *e.g.,* the call to stackFloatValue: (line 4 and 6). It also provides VM developers with a way to specify environment specific code (line 7 and 8). For example, the natural logarithm is implemented in the C standard library using the **log** function, while in Pharo, it is implemented using the **ln** message. Indeed, the **log** method identifier (*i.e.,* selector in Pharo's terminology) exists in Pharo but computes a base 10 logarithm.

Moreover, Pharo is a dynamically-typed language that does not use explicit type annotations. However, the Slang VM generator needs them to produce correct C code although the simulation ignores them (line 2). This means that wrong type annotations only impact the generation introduces issues specific to the generated VM. Notice that the semantic gaps are aggravated by additional Pharo features *e.g.,* inheritance, polymorphism, method redefinition, super message sends, block closures, managed memory, absence of stack allocation which require more complex code transformations.

2.3 Limits of Simulation-Based Testing

Simulation-based VM generator frameworks allow VM developers to debug and develop in a simulation environment. Simulation environments allow developers to apply automated unit testing on the VM. Let's consider for example the VM test case depicted in Listing 1.2. This test case is executed as plain Pharo code during simulation and passes, regardless of bugs in type annotations. If we modify or remove the type annotation, the generated VM does not work anymore: it casts a float to an int, producing unexpected results. Similar problems have been informally reported for simulation-based VM generator frameworks such as RPython [32].

```
1   testPrimitiveNaturalLogarithmShouldFailForNegativeNumber
2   | aFloat |
3   aFloat := self newFloatFromInt: −1.
4   interpreter push: aFloat.
5   interpreter primitiveNaturalLogarithm.
6   self assert: interpreter failed.
```

Listing 1.2. Excerpt of a test case validating that the logarithm of a negative number sets the interpreter in a failed state. This test cases passes in simulation but does not capture potential typing failures of the generated code.

2.4 Problem Statement

Problem. Simulation-based VM generators introduces semantic gaps due to the differences between the simulated and generated VM *e.g.,* semantic typing difference, memory management, integer semantics, etc. We have observed that in current state-of-the-art simulation-based VM generators, testing only the simulated VM is not enough.

Proposal. We propose to extend simulation-based VM generator frameworks to reuse simulation test cases by generating and executing them on generated VMs. We validate the outputs of both simulated and generated test cases using differential testing: a difference in the execution indicates a VM bug or a VM generator bug. However, test cases generated in such a way may also fall into semantic gaps similar to the ones found in the VM. To validate that our test case generation is correct, we propose to combine differential testing with non-semantic-preserving mutations.

We formulate the following research questions: **RQ1.** Does Test Transmutation detect semantic gaps between simulated and generated VMs? **RQ2.** Does Test Transmutation detect bugs in existing VM test cases?

3   Test Transmutation

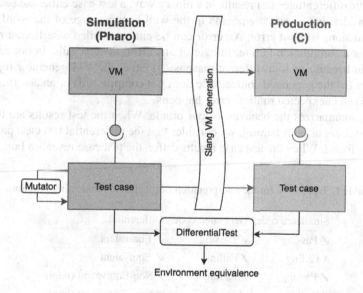

Fig. 1. Test Transmutation overview. We generate test cases with the VM and compare their results with differential testing. Mutations increase the number and variety of test cases.

We propose Test Transmutation a solution to address semantic gaps by generating the simulated VM's test cases (cf. Fig. 1). Existing simulation test cases are therefore reused to also test the generated VM. We execute both simulated and generated test cases and compare their results with differential testing [23] to detect execution differences. A core insight is that regardless of the differences between simulated and generated code, test cases are always self-validating and have a deterministic and discrete result: they either succeed, or they fail in an assertion check or a runtime error. Our differential testing process relies on this self-validating property to build the test oracle: two test cases have equivalent behavior if they both pass or if they both fail.

Generating the test cases presents two main challenges. First, generated test cases suffer from semantic gaps similar to the ones found in VMs. Second, the existing and maintained VM test cases will in general successfully execute, making them poor inputs for the differential testing process.

To address these challenges, we extend our approach with automatic non-semantic-preserving mutations [12]. Mutated test cases are expected to keep behaving similarly when executed in the simulated and generated VM. For example, if a mutated test case breaks in the simulated VM, it should also fails in the generated VM. A non-equivalence of test results shows that there is a bug in the VM or in the VM generator.

3.1 Differential Testing of Test Cases

We check for functional equivalence of both simulated and generated VMs by applying differential testing [23] and validating whether a test case has *similar* results in both. Our heuristic differentiates test results in a binary way: a test case either passes or fails.

We consider that a test case passes in the well-known usage of the word: It runs all its instructions without error. An error can be either: a failed assertion, a run-time exception or a compilation failure. In case of any error, the test fails. In our case, failures happen because of four different reasons: (i) either the VM generator rejects the program, or (ii) the generated source code does not compile, (iii) or an assertion check fails, or (iv) an unexpected runtime error happens.

Table 1 summarizes the behavior of our oracle. When the test results are the same (*i.e.,* both success or both failure), we consider that the differential test case passes and no bug was found. When the test case results differ, the test case reveals a bug.

Table 1. Truth table for the interpretation of the differential testing function.

Simulated code	Generated code	Differential
✓ Passing	✓ Passing	✓ Equivalent
✗ Failing	✗ Failing	✓ Equivalent
✓ Passing	✗ Failing	✗ Non-Equivalent (bug!)
✗ Failing	✓ Passing	✗ Non-Equivalent (bug!)

3.2 Test Case Variations with Non-Semantic-Preserving Mutations

Since we generate test cases from existing simulation test cases, the test cases suffer from similar semantic gaps as the VMs *e.g.,* typing semantics differences, as well as a few others *e.g.,* the testing framework. Moreover all have poor variations in their results because the VM is maintained to pass all test cases. We tackle this issue by applying non-semantics-preserving mutations on the available test cases. Mutations automate the creation of more inputs allowing one to gain confidence in the correctness of the generation process and the generated test cases. Our main observation here is that applying mutations to the original simulated test cases should keep the generated counterpart functionally equivalent. In other words, if a mutant breaks a simulated test case, we expect it to break the generated test case too. Similarly, if a mutant keeps a simulation test case passing, we expect the generated test case to be passing. Therefore we validate mutants with the same process of differential testing explained in the previous section.

We perform non-semantics-preserving mutations of the test cases passing in both environments [1]. For example, Listing 1.3 shows the application of the mutation operator *removeStatementMutation* which removes a statement from the method.

```
1   testScavengeNonSurvivorObjectShouldLeaveMemoryEmpty
2      self newNewSpaceObject.
3      "memory collectNewSpace. <- removed statement"
4      self assert: memory isEmpty
```

Listing 1.3. Example of an automatically mutated test case. The original test case allocates an object, executes a garbage collection and expects the memory to be freed. A mutation operator removes the garbage collection, making the assertion (line 4) fail.

4   Experimental Context of the Validation and Threats to Validity

We implemented Test Transmutation on top of the Pharo VM [7], an industrial-level VM used by the Pharo programming language, a continuation of the work performed in the OpenSmalltalk-VM. At the time of writing, the Pharo VM has around 1000 unit test cases [30] written in the simulation environment covering the memory manager, the bytecode interpreter, the language primitives, and the Just-In-Time compiler. These test cases are executed for simulations of different for simulations of word sizes (32/64 bits) and processor architectures (x86, x86-64, ARM32 and ARM64).

Selected Test Case Subset. Test cases are written in plain Pharo, thus their generation was not initially possible: test cases use many idioms not supported by the Slang VM generator such as the testing framework generation. Therefore, we focused on a subset of the available test cases, namely the memory management test cases. Such test cases cover the implementation of a generational scavenger garbage collector and a mark-compact collector for older objects [37] their structure and their allocation schemes.

The selected subset may be considered not representative of the entire VM process. To address this issue, Sect. 5 shows that our approach covers many semantic gaps that are independent of the tested component.

Testing Requires Disabling Optimizations The Slang VM generator is tailored for performance. In addition, many optimizations are required for a correct generation. For example, method inlining is required for stack-allocation to work as expected. Indeed, methods allocating stack-memory (*i.e.*, using alloca(), Sect. 5.1) need to be inlined in their caller, otherwise the allocated memory is freed right-away. Such optimizations affect the observability of the program, and need to be disabled to allow their testing. Thus, they pose a potential threat to validity. To minimize this threat to validity, we only disable inlines required by test cases.

5 Bug Detection Assessment

To evaluate the ability of Test Transmutation to detect bugs (**RQ1**), we manually introduce bugs in the VM based on bugs experimented by VM developers in the past. We
then evaluate those bugs on 238 test cases covering the modified code. This section
presents the introduced bugs, their rationale, relevance and reports the observed the
outputs. This section shows that Test Transmutation detects semantic gaps between
simulated and generated VMs.

Our results show that our approach is able to unveil several differences between
the simulated and generated VMs. We consider as a correct behavior that the
Slang VM generator rejects problematic code during generation time. However, our
evaluation shows that the Slang VM generator presents the following flaws that are
presented in the remainder of this section:

Memory Management. Careless memory management produces runtime failures.

Type annotations. Errors in type annotations may produce runtime failures.

Name Conflicts. Name conflicts creates compile-time errors.

Undefined Behavior. The Slang VM generator is unaware of the target language undefined behavior. Therefore the generated code may exhibit undefined behavior.

Unsupported Simulation. Some programs are invalid at simulation time, although they
can be generated and executed correctly.

5.1 Memory Management Differences

Background. The simulation running in Pharo presents deep differences with the target
C runtime environment in terms of memory management. Indeed, Pharo is a managed
language with garbage collection and no explicit stack allocation, while C allows developers to perform stack allocations by using standard library functions such as alloca().
This means that the developers should take special care when simulating manual memory management while developing the VM memory manager. An example of such a
simulation is illustrated in Listing 1.4.

```
1  alloca: desiredSize
2     memory := self generatedCode: [ self alloca: desiredSize ]. " stack allocation "
3              simulationCode: [ ByteArray new: desiredSize ]. " heap allocation "
```

Listing 1.4. Example of simulation specific code simulating stack-allocation with heap allocation.

Bug Description. Stack allocations are simulated as simple heap allocations. This
means that simulated stack allocations out-live their defining stack-frames, allowing
programs to freely access and modify such a piece of memory. The bug introduced
memory accesses to stack-allocated regions returned to their caller. **Results.** All simulated test cases passed, whereas all generated test cases failed with segmentation faults.

5.2 Type Annotation Errors

Background. Simulated and generated VMs present differences in typing. On the one
hand, the simulated VM executes on top of Pharo and uses its dynamically-typed features. On the other hand, generating the VM to C requires the VM source code to

have some type annotation. Moreover, even though type annotations are available in the source code, they are ignored by the simulation environment. An example of such type annotations is illustrated in Listing 1.5.

```
1  addGCRoot: varLoc
2    "<var: #varLoc type: #'long int *'> ### Original annotation"
3    <var: #varLoc type: #'char *'> "### Buggy replacement"
4    extraRootCount >= ExtraRootsSize ifTrue: [ ↑ false ]. "out of space"
5    extraRootCount := extraRootCount + 1.
6    extraRoots at: extraRootCount put: varLoc.
7    ↑true
```

Listing 1.5. Example of type Annotation Error

Bug Description. Wrong or missing type annotations break the generation process or make the executable VMs produce runtime errors. The introduced bug is a change of a type annotation from a long int pointer to a char pointer.

Results. All simulated test cases passed, whereas all generated test cases failed with segmentation faults. We consider this a VM generator bug.

5.3   Literal Type Errors

Background. Another simulated vs generated VMs typing error happens during type checking and type inference at generation-time. The VM generation process performs type inference to guide generation.

Bug Description. We introduced a bug by changing the type of a literal from integer to float with the same value as illustrated in Listing 1.6.

```
1  weakArrayFormat
2    "↑4 ### Original code"
3    ↑4.0 "### Buggy replacement"
```

Listing 1.6. Bug introduced by changing the type of a literal from integer to float.

Results

Modifying a literal's type had an effect both in the simulated and generated test cases. 10 out of 238 test cases failed on the simulation because the Float class does not implement the message #bitAnd:. At the same time, none of the test cases could be generated because VM generation eagerly rejected them with a type error.

Notice that we consider this the correct behavior: generated test cases detect the difference, in this case at VM-generation time.

5.4   Name Conflicts and Name Mangling

Background. The simulated and the generation target environment do not have the same rules for name management. For example, it is perfectly valid in the simulation (written in Pharo) to have a method and a class' attribute with the same name. However, in C a function and a global variable with the same name produce name conflicts. This difference is aggravated by the fact that the Pharo convention dictates that getters and setters have the same name as the attributes they access.

Bug Description. We introduced a bug by explicitly preventing the inlining of a getter and setter pair as shown in Listing 1.7.

```
1  bogon
2    <inlineInC: #false>
3    ↑ bogon
```

Listing 1.7. Example of non-inlined getter, creating a name conflict on generation.

Results. All these being valid Pharo idioms, simulated test cases remain passing. However, the VM generation process accepts this idiom but generates wrong C code, causing an ulterior compilation error. We consider this a VM generator bug: the VM-generator should manage the name-mangling of methods and generate a working VM.

5.5   Undefined Behavior

Background. The C programming language targeted by the Slang VM generator contains 193 undefined behavior in C99 [11]. Upon encountering an undefined behavior, C compilers are able to apply aggressive optimization. Thus, C developers must avoid writing them in their program. However, since VM developers write mainly code in the simulation environment, both the developer and the Slang VM generator should make sure to not produce code with undefined behavior.

Bug Description. We introduced a C undefined behavior by introducing an arithmetic overflow (Listing 1.8).

```
1  howManyFreeObjects
2    | counter |
3    counter := 0.
4    self allFreeObjectsDo: [ :freeObject | counter := counter + 1 ].
5    "↑ counter ### Original code"
6    ↑ counter + self maxCInteger + 1 " ### Buggy replacement"
```

Listing 1.8. Introducing a potential cause of undefined behavior .

Results. Since in Pharo, integer arithmetics is potentially unbound, the expression self maxCInteger + 1 is automatically coerced to a large precision integer, making 5 simulation test cases fail. At the same time, all 238 generated test cases pass in the generation target environments. We consider this a Slang VM generator bug: either the program should be rejected by the Slang VM generator, or the simulation environment should be modified to have the same integer arithmetics as the target.

5.6   External Functions and Name-mangling

Background. The Slang VM generator allows any function or method to call any external C function by just mangling method-invocation selectors to C function names at generation time. However, the Slang VM generator's name mangling can produce the same function name for different method selectors. Moreover, to enable simulation of external functions, a simulation specific implementation requires to be provided. Thus, VM developers must use the correct method invocation so a function call works on both simulated and generated code.

Bug Description. We introduced a bug by replacing an external function call with an equivalent one from the name mangling point of view (Listing 1.9).

```
1   "Original code"
2   self me: destAddress mc: sourceAddress py: bytes
3
4   "Buggy replacement"
5   self memc: destAddress p: sourceAddress y: bytes
```

Listing 1.9. Example changing a call to the C function memcpy by a version that generates correct code but cannot be properly simulated.

Results. This modification produced 50 failing simulated test cases, while all 238 generated test cases passed. We consider this a VM-generator bug: the simulation should have been allowed to run or the VM-generator should have rejected the program.

6 Empirical Results on the Pharo VM

To evaluate the capability of Test Transmutation to find bugs in existing test cases (**RQ2**), we apply our approach on a subset of the existing VM test cases. This section shows that Test Transmutation is able to detect bugs in existing VM test cases.

6.1 Test Case Characterization

Our validation executes Test Transmutation on a subset of 256 tests, out of which 238 are correctly generated by our prototype implementation. We categorize the test cases as follow:

Memory structure. Test cases checking that the memory structural properties. For example, they check that Garbage Collection specific variables are initialized.

Memory allocation. Test cases checking the multiple object allocation heuristics in the VM heap. For example, they check that creating a new object reduces the space available in the new space.

New space garbage collection. Test cases checking the copy garbage collector used in the new space. For example, they check that allocating two objects in a row, should allocate both objects next to one another.

Old space garbage collection. Test cases checking the mark compact algorithm used for old generation garbage collection. For example, they check that objects referenced are marked, and not reclaimed nor moved by the garbage collection.

6.2   Prototype Results

Table 2 reports on the test cases generation status. The test cases are executed on Pharo 9 to test the Pharo 9 VM. Currently all 256 initial test cases are passing in the simulation. Of those 256, 238 are passing in the generated VM for Ubuntu 20.0 and x64.

From the existing 238 test cases we generate a total 494 mutants. The mutants are generated by using coverage directed mutant creations to only create mutants that are in the path of at least one test case. The execution of the test cases also uses coverage information to only execute necessary test cases for each mutant. Every executed test case for each mutant is executed in both the simulated and generated VM. There was 1890 test case executions to validate the 494 generated mutants.

Table 2. Detailed categorization of the test cases considered and relevant statistics.

Category	Sub-Category 1	Passing test case in simulated VM	Passing test case in generated VM	Mutant executions	Mutant detecting bugs
Memory	New space	8	7	7	0
Structure	Old space	7	1	1	0
Memory	Allocation in new space	9	8	13	0
Allocation	Allocation in old space	21	21	71	0
	Allocation strategies	127	127	1464	2
New space	GC of regular objects	38	29	62	11
Garbage collection	GC of weak objects	9	9	34	0
	GC of ephemeron objects	19	19	101	10
Old space	GC of regular objects	9	8	33	0
Garbage collection	GC of unmovable object	9	9	104	0
Total		256	238	1890	23

6.3   Result Analysis

Since the VM has been used industrially for several years now, the VM is stable and we expect to find few bugs in the code. However, in the current prototype implementation we detect three kinds of bugs captured using 23 mutated test cases.

Stack Allocation Issues. At first, Test Transmutation uncovered the alloca simulation issue described in Sect. 5.1. Non-inlined stack allocations are freed as soon as the allocating function returns, causing memory access violations in all tests. We had to fix this bug in order to obtain these results and the following bugs.

Division Differences. Mutations unveil a difference in the behavior between simulated and generated VMs regarding integer division. In Pharo both the selector #// and #/ exists. The first is returning an exact integer whereas the second is returning a fraction. Moreover, #// truncates the result of the division, and returns an integer. Both selectors are generating the / operator in C. Mutants break an implicit invariant of the VM, creating a runtime error in the simulated VM.

Runtime Assertion Differences. Mutations unveil a difference in the behavior between simulated and generated VMs regarding runtime assertions. Runtime assertions check for invariants to eagerly prevent complex scenarios such as memory corruptions. On the one hand, invariant assertions in the simulated VM stop the execution and fail test cases. On the other hand, invariant assertions in the generated VM log an error and continue the execution. Because of these differences, 21 mutated test cases are passing in the simulated VM but not in the generated VM.

7   Related Work

Simulation-based VM generator frameworks are VM specific compilers: they generate VMs from a specification to an executable form, applying VM specific transformations and optimizations. In this sense, this section also presents compiler testing approaches that are related to ours.

Differential Compiler Testing. Differential testing was introduced by McKeeman [23]. The author shows the effectiveness of differential testing on C compilers to find bugs. They generate random test cases ex-nihilo in different ways, depending on the level they test (e.g. sequence syntactically correct C program or Type-correct C program). On the one hand, we also apply differential testing to uncover differences between two execution environments, in our case a simulation and a generation target environment. On the other hand, we do not use random test cases: we start from existing test cases and apply non-semantic-preserving mutations on them.

CSmith [41] expands on previous work to generate random C programs free of undefined behavior. They describe their generated programs as having no need for an oracle. They apply the generated program with a cross-compiler differential testing strategy. Our work does not require to generate programs free of undefined behavior, since the simulation environment has no undefined behavior. It allows us to detect when the VM-generator introduces undefined behavior in the generated VM.

Equivalence Modulo Input. Equivalence Modulo Input (EMI) proposes to create functionally equivalent test input programs. Those test input programs are created by applying mutations on dead code [21,22] or semantic-preserving mutations on live code [35]. The mutated programs are expected to be functionally equivalent to the initial program. Therefore, they check that the observable behavior is equivalent between the original program and the mutated program. The mutated programs are designed to not introduce new undefined behavior. This works under the assumption that the initial program does not contain undefined behavior. Our solution applies non-semantic-preserving mutation on live code instead.

Mutation-Based Test Assessments. Many works use mutation-based approaches to measure the effectiveness and efficiency of testing techniques [27]. Similar to us, many works use automated mutations to guide test case generation [14,16,28]. Papadakis et al. [27] identify that many approaches present type I errors because of the subsumed mutant threat, that creates irrelevant mutants that inflate mutant scores and skew results, altering conclusions. Such threat does not apply to our work, because we only use mutants to generate new test cases and we do not compare two testing approaches nor measure mutation scores.

Mutation-Based Simulation Testing. Several work have applied mutations on simulation-based models outside of VMs. Rutherford et al. [33] present an automated approach on top of distributed system simulations using mutations. Aichernig et al. [2–4] present a mutation-testing approach for UML models. To the best of our knowledge, Test Transmutation is the first approach applying mutation-based testing for VMs code, and VM simulation environments.

Dealing With Semantic Gaps. PharoJS [8] validates application generation from Pharo to Javascript with the application test cases. It uses cross compiler differential testing, comparing the Pharo and Javascript compiler. It also uses a different implementation in which the Pharo environment executes the test case and is sending messages to the Javascript environment rather than compiling the test cases to Javascript and then executing them. Moreover PharoJS test cases do not rely on mutations.

Also, rather than creating semantic gaps, some prefer removing it [6]. Besnard et al. unify the semantics of a model for execution, deployment and tooling. They implement a VM to run the executable model. This VM allows them to control remotely the execution, allowing tooling such as debuggers.

8   Conclusion

This paper describes a novel technique to test simulation-based VM generator frameworks we call Test Transmutation. It extends simulation-based VM generator frameworks to support the generation of test cases, to then apply differential testing between simulated and generated VMs. It reuses existing simulation test cases, if any are available. We apply non-semantic-preserving mutations to increment test variability and minimize the impact of semantic gaps introduced during test generation. We apply our prototype implementation on the Pharo VM and validate it by manually introducing bugs inspired from VM developers and by executing it on real test cases. Our evaluation shows that our approach detects typical bugs and detects bugs and translation differences on a an industrially-used VM that is stable and has many users.

In the future we plan to investigate Test Transmutation on JIT compiler test cases, to use with VM specific mutations derived from commits the history, and to compare the different generated VM.

Acknowledgement. This work was supported by Ministry of Higher Education and Research, Hauts de France Regional Council and the AlaMVic Action Exploratoire INRIA - Lille Nord Europe.

References

1. Abdi, M., Rocha, H., Demeyer, S.: test amplification in the Pharo Smalltalk ecosystem. In: International Workshop on Smalltalk Technologies (IWST), August 2019. shorturl.at/floF4
2. Aichernig, B.K., et al.: Model-based mutation testing of an industrial measurement device. In: Seidl, M., Tillmann, N. (eds.) TAP 2014. LNCS, vol. 8570, pp. 1–19. Springer, Cham (2014). https://doi.org/10.1007/978-3-319-09099-3_1
3. Aichernig, B.K., Brandl, H., Jöbstl, E., Krenn, W.: Efficient mutation killers in action. In: 2011 Fourth IEEE International Conference on Software Testing, Verification and Validation, pp. 120–129 (2011). https://doi.org/10.1109/ICST.2011.57

4. Aichernig, B.K., Brandl, H., Jöbstl, E., Krenn, W., Schlick, R., Tiran, S.: Killing strategies for model-based mutation testing. Softw. Test. Verif. Reliab. **25**(8), 716–748 (2015)
5. Alpern, B., et al.: Experiences porting the jikes rvm to linux/ia32. In: Java Virtual Machine Research and Technology Symposium, pp. 51–64 (2002)
6. Besnard, V., Brun, M., Dhaussy, P., Jouault, F., Olivier, D., Teodorov, C.: Towards one model interpreter for both design and deployment. In: Third International Workshop on Executable Modeling (EXE 2017), September 2017. https://hal.archives-ouvertes.fr/hal-01585318
7. Black, A.P., Ducasse, S., Nierstrasz, O., Pollet, D., Cassou, D., Denker, M.: Pharo by Example. Square Bracket Associates, Kehrsatz, Switzerland (2009). http://books.pharo.org
8. Bouraqadi, N., Mason, D.: Mocks, proxies, and transpilation as development strategies for web development. In: Proceedings of the 11th edition of the International Workshop on Smalltalk Technologies, pp. 1–6. IWST 2016, Association for Computing Machinery, August 2016. http://www.esug.org/data/ESUG2016/IWST/Papers/IWST_2016_paper_23.pdf
9. Casey, K., Gregg, D., Ertl, M.A.: Tiger – an interpreter generation tool. In: Bodik, R. (ed.) CC 2005. LNCS, vol. 3443, pp. 246–249. Springer, Heidelberg (2005). https://doi.org/10.1007/978-3-540-31985-6_18
10. Chen, J., et al.: A survey of compiler testing. ACM Comput. Surv. **53**(1), 1–36 (2020). https://dl.acm.org/doi/10.1145/3363562
11. Commitee, C.S.: C99 specification (2007). shorturl.at/goyJQ
12. DeMillo, R.A., Lipton, R.J., Sayward, F.G.: Program mutation: a new approach to program testing. Infotech State Art Report Softw. Testing **2**(1979), 107–126 (1979)
13. Ertl, M.A., Gregg, D.: Optimizing indirect branch prediction accuracy in virtual machine interpreters. In: Proceedings of the ACM SIGPLAN 2003 Conference on Programming Language Design and Implementation, pp. 278–288 (2003)
14. Fraser, G., Zeller, A.: Mutation-driven generation of unit tests and oracles. IEEE Trans. Softw. Eng. **38**(2), 278–292 (2012). https://doi.org/10.1109/TSE.2011.93
15. Gregg, D., Ertl, M.A.: A language and tool for generating efficient virtual machine interpreters. In: Lengauer, C., Batory, D., Consel, C., Odersky, M. (eds.) Domain-Specific Program Generation. LNCS, vol. 3016, pp. 196–215. Springer, Heidelberg (2004). https://doi.org/10.1007/978-3-540-25935-0_12
16. Harman, M., Jia, Y., Langdon, W.B.: Strong higher order mutation-based test data generation. In: Proceedings of the 19th ACM SIGSOFT Symposium and the 13th European Conference on Foundations of Software Engineering, pp. 212–222. ESEC/FSE 2011, Association for Computing Machinery, New York (2011). https://doi.org/10.1145/2025113.2025144
17. Hölzle, U., Chambers, C., Ungar, D.: Optimizing dynamically-typed object-oriented languages with polymorphic inline caches. In: America, P. (ed.) ECOOP 1991. LNCS, vol. 512, pp. 21–38. Springer, Heidelberg (1991). https://doi.org/10.1007/BFb0057013
18. Ingalls, D., Kaehler, T., Maloney, J., Wallace, S., Kay, A.: Back to the future: the story of squeak, a practical smalltalk written in itself. In: Proceedings of Object-Oriented Programming, Systems, Languages, and Applications conference (OOPSLA 1997), pp. 318–326. ACM Press, November 1997. https://doi.org/10.1145/263700.263754
19. Just, R., Jalali, D., Inozemtseva, L., Ernst, M.D., Holmes, R., Fraser, G.: Are mutants a valid substitute for real faults in software testing? In: Proceedings of the 22nd ACM SIGSOFT International Symposium on Foundations of Software Engineering, pp. 654–665 (2014)
20. Kotselidis, C., Nisbet, A., Zakkak, F.S., Foutris, N.: Cross-ISA debugging in meta-circular VMs. In: Proceedings of International Workshop on Virtual Machines and Intermediate Languages (VMIL 2017), pp. 1–9 (2017). https://doi.org/10.1145/3141871.3141872
21. Le, V., Afshari, M., Su, Z.: Compiler validation via equivalence modulo inputs. In: Programming Language Design and Implementation, PLDI 2014 (2014). https://doi.org/10.1145/2594291.2594334

22. Le, V., Sun, C., Su, Z.: Finding deep compiler bugs via guided stochastic program mutation. ACM SIGPLAN Notices **50**, 386–399 (2015). https://doi.org/10.1145/2858965.2814319
23. McKeeman, W.M.: Differential testing for software. Digital Tech. J. **10**, 100–107 (1998)
24. Miranda, E.: The cog smalltalk virtual machine. In: Proceedings of VMIL 2011 (2011)
25. Miranda, E., Béra, C., Boix, E.G., Ingalls, D.: Two decades of smalltalk vm development: live vm development through simulation tools. In: Proceedings of International Workshop on Virtual Machines and Intermediate Languages (VMIL 2018), pp. 57–66. ACM (2018). https://doi.org/10.1145/3281287.3281295
26. Misse-Chanabier, P., Aranega, V., Polito, G., Ducasse, S.: Illicium a modular transpilation toolchain from Pharo to c. In: International workshop of Smalltalk Technologies. Köln, Germany, August 2019
27. Papadakis, M., Henard, C., Harman, M., Jia, Y., Le Traon, Y.: Threats to the validity of mutation-based test assessment. In: Proceedings of the 25th International Symposium on Software Testing and Analysis, pp. 354–365. ISSTA 2016, Association for Computing Machinery, New York (2016). https://doi.org/10.1145/2931037.2931040
28. Papadakis, M., Malevris, N.: Automatic mutation test case generation via dynamic symbolic execution. In: 2010 IEEE 21st International Symposium on Software Reliability Engineering, pp. 121–130 (2010). https://doi.org/10.1109/ISSRE.2010.38
29. Person, S., Dwyer, M.B., Elbaum, S., Păsăreanu, C.S.: Differential symbolic execution. In: Proceedings of the 16th ACM SIGSOFT International Symposium on Foundations of Software Engineering, pp. 226–237. SIGSOFT 2008/FSE-16, Association for Computing Machinery, November 2008. https://doi.org/10.1145/1453101.1453131
30. Polito, G., et al.: Cross-ISA testing of the Pharo VM: lessons learned while porting to ARMv8. In: MPLR, Germany. Münster, Germany, September 2021. https://doi.org/10.1145/3475738.3480715
31. Rigo, A., Pedroni, S.: PyPy's approach to virtual machine construction. In: Proceedings of the 2006 conference on Dynamic languages symposium, ACM, New York (2006)
32. RPythonCommunity: Rpython documentation on test translation (2016). shorturl.at/gBDGT
33. Rutherford, M., Carzaniga, A., Wolf, A.: Evaluating test suites and adequacy criteria using simulation-based models of distributed systems. Softw. Eng. IEEE Trans. **34**, 452–470 (2008). https://doi.org/10.1109/TSE.2008.33
34. Simon, D., Cifuentes, C., Cleal, D., Daniels, J., White, D.: Java on the bare metal of wireless sensor devices: the Squawk Java virtual machine. In: VEE 2006: Proceedings of the 2nd International Conference on Virtual Execution Environments, pp. 78–88. ACM Press, New York (2006). https://doi.org/10.1145/1134760.1134773
35. Sun, C., Le, V., Su, Z.: Finding compiler bugs via live code mutation. In: Proceedings of the 2016 ACM SIGPLAN International Conference on Object-Oriented Programming, Systems, Languages, and Applications, pp. 849–863. OOPSLA 2016, Association for Computing Machinery, October 2016. https://doi.org/10.1145/2983990.2984038
36. Terekhov, A.A., Verhoef, C.: The realities of language conversions. IEEE Softw. **17**(6), 111–124 (2000). https://doi.org/10.1109/52.895180
37. Ungar, D.: Generation scavenging: a non-disruptive high performance storage reclamation algorithm. ACM SIGPLAN Notices **19**(5) (1984). https://doi.org/10.1145/390011.808261
38. Ungar, D., Spitz, A., Ausch, A.: Constructing a metacircular virtual machine in an exploratory programming environment. In: Companion to Object-Oriented Programming, Systems, Languages, and Applications Conference (OOPSLA 2005), ACM (2005)
39. Wimmer, C., Haupt, M., Vanter, M.L.V.D., Jordan, M., Daynes, L., Simon, D.: Maxine: an approachable virtual machine for, and in, java. Technical Report 2012–0098, Oracle Labs (2012)

40. Würthinger, T., et al.: One VM to rule them all. In: International Symposium on New Ideas, New Paradigms, and Reflections on Programming & Software (ONWARD 2013) (2013)
41. Yang, X., Chen, Y., Eide, E., Regehr, J.: Finding and understanding bugs in C compilers. In: Programming Language Design and Implementation. PLDI 2011 (2011). https://doi.org/10. 1145/1993498.1993532

SEED: Semantic Graph Based Deep Detection for Type-4 Clone

Zhipeng Xue, Zhijie Jiang$^{(\boxtimes)}$, Chenlin Huang$^{(\boxtimes)}$, Rulin Xu, Xiangbing Huang, and Liumin Hu

National University of Defense Technology, Changsha, China
{xuezhipeng19,jiangzhijie,clhuang,xurulin11}@nudt.edu.cn

Abstract. Type-4 clones refer to a pair of code snippets with similar semantics but written in different syntax, which challenges the existing code clone detection techniques. Previous studies, however, highly rely on syntactic structures and textual tokens, which cannot precisely represent the semantic information of code and might introduce non-negligible noise into the detection models. To overcome these limitations, we design a novel semantic graph-based deep detection approach, called SEED. For a pair of code snippets, SEED constructs a semantic graph of each code snippet based on intermediate representation to represent the code semantic more precisely compared to the representations based on lexical and syntactic analysis. To accommodate the characteristics of Type-4 clones, a semantic graph is constructed focusing on the operators and API calls instead of all tokens. Then, SEED generates the feature vectors by using the graph match network and performs clone detection based on the similarity among the vectors. Extensive experiments show that our approach significantly outperforms two baseline approaches over two public datasets and one customized dataset. Especially, SEED outperforms other baseline methods by an average of 25.2% in the form of F1-Score. Our experiments demonstrate that SEED can reach state-of-the-art and be useful for Type-4 clone detection in practice.

Keywords: Intelligent software engineering · Clone detection · Semantic graph · Graph neural network

1 Introduction

Code clones, widely existing in software systems (*e.g.*, 15%–25% in Linux kernel [1]), exert a significant impact on software maintenance and evolution (*e.g.*, fault localization [8,23] and code refactor [10,13]). Typically, code clones can be categorized into four types [14] based on different levels of similarity. **Type-4 clone** refers to syntactically dissimilar code snippets that implement the same semantic, which is the most challenging problem for traditional code clone detection techniques.

Currently, researchers have tried to consider Type-4 code clone detection as a classification task and solve it with deep learning methods [19,22]. They build

© Springer Nature Switzerland AG 2022
G. Perrouin et al. (Eds.): ICSR 2022, LNCS 13297, pp. 120–137, 2022.
https://doi.org/10.1007/978-3-031-08129-3_8

contextual embedding models of source code, form feature vectors for code representation, and then measure similarity among code vectors to detect code clones. For example, ASTNN [22] presents a two-stage embedding approach based on recurrent neural network (RNN) to extract features from the abstract syntax tree (AST). TBCCD [20] likely links the AST with tokens to add more semantic information and generates the feature vector by tree-based LSTM. The performances of those approaches, however, are limited due to the following two main limitations. First, the existing studies rely heavily on syntactic structures (*e.g.*, AST) and cannot precisely represent the semantic information of code. Second, textual tokens commonly adopted for the code representation do not contain semantics that Type-4 clones require but introduce unnecessary noise data.

To explore an effective semantic-based solution for Type-4 clones, we propose a novel approach called **SEED** (**S**emantic-based cod**E** clon**E** **D**etector) in this paper. The key idea of SEED is to perform clone detection based on 1) the code semantic structures rather than syntactic or lexical structures, and 2) emphasizing operator and API call tokens rather than universal tokens. First, SEED takes a code pair as input and constructs the semantic graph of each code based on intermediate representation (IR) [5,21] to represent the semantics of the source code. As the intermediary between high-level and assembly language, IR represents code as specific instructions and therefore is closer to the code semantics. Then, SEED models the semantic graphs by using the graph match network (GMN) [6] and generates feature vectors of source code. Finally, SEED predicts Type-4 clone pairs based on the similarities among feature vectors. We evaluate the performance of our approach compared with two typical baseline approaches over two public datasets and one large-scale customized dataset. The results prove that SEED outperforms baseline approaches by over 25.2% on average (reaching state-of-the-art) in the real-world scenario.

The main contributions of this paper are summarized as follows:

- we proposed a semantic-based deep learning approach SEED for Type-4 clone detection. SEED adopts the graph match network on the semantic graph, which is built from code semantic structures and enhanced by operator and API call tokens.
- We customized a Type-4 code clone dataset called CF-500[1] to mitigate the threat posed by the lack of semantics of popular datasets (i.e., POJ-104 and BigCloneBench). CF-500 consists of 500 functionalities, which is approximately 5 times the size of popular datasets.
- We evaluated the performance of our approach over two public datasets and one customized dataset. The results indicate that SEED can achieve state-of-the-art performance and outperforms baseline approaches by over 25.2% on average in a real-world scenario.

The remainder of this paper is organized as follows. In Sect. 2 we survey the related work about code clone detection. In Sect. 3, we illustrate the overview of SEED. In Sect. 4, we evaluate the performance of our approach with baselines

---

[1] https://github.com/xzpxzp123123/SEED.

by answering three research questions. In Sect. 5, we discuss the threats to the validity of the results. In Sect. 6, we conclude our work.

2   Related Work

As a critical problem in software maintenance, code clone detection has always been a hot spot for research. Traditional code clone detection approaches mainly focus on Type-1, 2, 3 code clones. They detect the code clone based on specific features such as tokens, metrics, and graphs. For example, sourcerer [9] performs clone detection based on the token. It obtains the code blocks with the least frequent tokens in code snippets, then indexes the code blocks and compares the blocks to find the clone pairs. Moreover, some methods use structure features such as AST, PDG, or CFG. Deckard [4] computes the feature vectors of ASTs and adopts the Locality Sensitive Hashing algorithm to detect cloned code. CCgraph [25] converts the code snippets into PDGs, it then applies the Weisfeiler-Lehman kernel to compute the graph similarity and identifies the clone pairs. Although these methods use various information of the code, the significant information loss in feature generation leads to the limitation of their performance. Also, these methods rely heavily on syntax information, which makes them unable to handle Type-4 code clones.

Since the deep learning perform impressive increment in natural language process, recently, researchers try to introduce deep learning in code clone detection. Different from traditional code clone detection approaches, the deep learning based code clone detection approaches convert the code feature into vector, and compare the similarity of the vectors. The deep learning based code clone detection approaches assign different weights to different parts of the code feature, which lead to a better performance on Type-4 code clone detection, White et al. [19] firstly introduces the deep learning method to code clone detection. They use a recurrent neural network to convert the textual information into the vector and learn the code representation from AST. Following this work, CDLH [18] and TBCCD [20] search for deep learning models that are more suitable for the tree structure of the AST and propose their method which uses the tree-based deep learning model to handle AST. ASTNN [22] proposes a novel two-step approach to represent the code snippet, using RNN to encode the AST of each statement first and transforming the AST encoding of all the statements into one vector to represent the code snippet. Oreo [15] and Deepsim [24] collect more than 20 features from code syntax, and transfer the collected features into vector. However, prior studies mainly relied on syntactic structure, as well as identifiers, leads to significant limitations in their performance on Type-4 clone detection. In contrast, SEED focuses on the semantic structure of code and the operator and API call tokens.

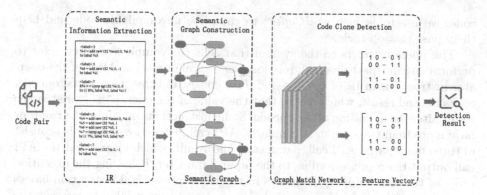

Fig. 1. The overview of SEED

3 Proposed Method

In this section, we propose a semantic-based deep graph learning method named SEED to cope with Type-4 clone detection. SEED detects Type-4 clones by constructing semantic graphs to represent code semantics while focusing on the operation semantics including operator and API call tokens.

3.1 Overview

Figure 1 shows the overview of SEED. SEED consists of three steps, semantic feature extraction, semantic graph construction, and code clone detection. During the first step, SEED takes a pair of code snippets as input and obtains the intermediate representation (IR) from the compiler. Then, in the second step, SEED constructs a semantic graph for each code snippet from IR to represent the code semantics. In the last step, SEED takes the semantic graphs as the input and transforms them into feature vectors using graph match network (GMN) [6]. Subsequently, SEED predicts Type-4 clones based on whether the cosine similarity between the two feature vectors reaches a certain threshold.

3.2 Semantic Feature Extraction

SEED is designed to detect Type-4 clones based on code semantics. IR, as the language between the high-level programming language and the assembly language, converts the complex grammars of the code into basic instructions. Therefore, this version is closer to the developer's intention and can represent the code semantics more precisely.

In this paper, SEED supports *C/C++* and *Java* and extracts semantic features using $LLVM^2$ and $Soot^3$. Since IR can only be generated from Compilable

---

2 https://llvm.org/.
3 http://soot-oss.github.io/soot/.

code, we use tools such as *JCoffee*[4] to complete uncompilable code and help them pass that obstacle.

The operator refers to the symbol that tells the compiler or interpreter to perform specific mathematical, relational or logical operation. Most of the operator instructions in IR of *C/C++* and *Java* consist of three main parts: opcode, operand, and result, which means that the value of the operand is stored in the result after the operation of the opcode. Some instructions may miss the result or have more than two operands. Similarly, API call instructions in IR also consist of three main parts: API call, parameter, and result, which means that the API call output the result according to the input parameter. Following the execution order of the code snippet, IR divides instructions into several instruction blocks according to the branch instruction (i.e., br) and uses a label to present the entry of each block. For example, Fig. 2(b) shows the IR for the source code in Fig. 2(a). Line 11 in Fig. 2(b) indicates that the sum of %sum.0 and %i.0 is stored in %4. Compared with token-based and AST-based Type-4 code clone detectors [2,9], instructions in IR focus on the operations on the variable, which describe the process of code execution and represent the intention of the developer (i.e., code semantics).

3.3   Semantic Graph Construction

To represent the code semantics, SEED combines the data flow and control flow to form the semantic graph based on IR while focusing on operator and API call tokens. In this section, we introduce semantic graph construction from two aspects: nodes and edges.

Node. Different from previous studies [18–20], which leverages all the textual tokens, the semantic graph constructed in this section only contains data type, operator, and API call tokens. We do not introduce identifier tokens in the semantic graph, since the identifier tokens in code are not reliable, the same identifier tokens can represent different semantics and lead to imprecise semantic representation in clone detection. In contrast, the same operator and API call tokens perform the same semantics in different codes.

Since each instruction contains only one operation (*i.e.*, one operator or one API call), we extract the operation from each instruction and take it as the node of the semantic graph. Since the label in IR represents the entry of each instruction block and contains the information of the control dependency of the code snippets, SEED also introduces the label as the node. Moreover, to maintain the code semantics, SEED considers the constant and input data. If the operand of an instruction is a constant, we add a constant node next to its operation node. If the operand is input data, we add an input node with its data type.

For example, as shown in Fig. 2(a) and Fig. 2(b), the line for (int i = n; i > 0; i−−) in the source code includes three components: int i=0, i>0, and

---

[4] https://github.com/piyush69/JCoffee.

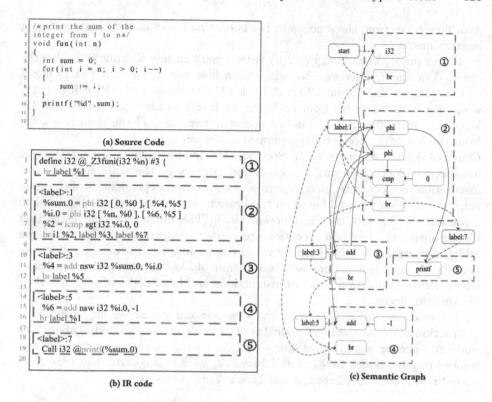

(a) Source Code

(b) IR code

(c) Semantic Graph

Fig. 2. An illustrative example of a source code snippet and its corresponding IR code and semantic graph

i−−. Accordingly, the compiler splits the line into three different IR instructions in line 6, line 7 and line 15 of Fig. 2(b). These operations on variable i include phi, cmp, and add. SEED takes these three operations as three nodes. Similarly, the line printf("%d", sum) in Fig. 2(a) is recognized as a API call by compiler, and compiler generates corresponding IR instructions in line 19 of Fig. 2(b). SEED extracts the API call printf and adds an operation node. For the constant 0 in the instruction of line 7, we add a constant node 0 next to the operation cmp. Moreover, instructions in lines 4, 10, 14 and 18 represent the labels in IR, and SEED takes them as label nodes. The variable n in the instruction of line 1 represents the input data; thus, SEED adds a node i32 to the semantic graph.

Edge. To integrate the data dependency and the control dependency, we add the data flow edge and the control flow edge to the semantic graph.

Data Flow. For each instruction, if the result of it performs as the operand or parameter of another, we connect operation nodes of these two instructions with a data flow edge. Moreover, for each constant node or input node, we connect the data flow edges from these nodes to the operation nodes of their corresponding instructions.

For example, %sum.0 in Fig. 2(b) is the result in line 5, while it is also the operand in line 7. Therefore, we add a data flow edge from node phi in line 5 to node cmp in line 7. Since %sum.0 is also the parameter of API call printf, we add a data flow edge from node phi in line 5 to node printf in line 19. Moreover, since 0 is the operand of operator cmp, we add the data flow edge from the constant node 0 to the operator node cmp in line 7.

Control Flow. As discussed in Sect. 3.2, IR divides instructions into several instruction blocks following the execution process of the code snippet. The instruction blocks can be used to represent the control dependencies of the code snippet. They are divided based on the branch instruction and use the label to represent the entry of each instruction block. The jumps between instruction blocks during the program execution are guided by operator br. Therefore, we add the control flow edge from br to corresponding label nodes. To illustrate the affiliation of instructions and instruction blocks, we also add control flow edges between operation nodes of instructions and label nodes of corresponding instruction blocks.

For example, in Fig. 2(b), since the operator add and br belong to the same instruction block as the label node label:3, we connect the node label:3 to node add and br with control flow edges. Moreover, since node br in line 8 is related to label nodes label:3 and label:7, we add a control flow edge from node br to label nodes label:3 and label:7, respectively.

3.4   Code Clone Detection

SEED takes the clone detection task as a matching task. For a pair of code snippets, SEED generates the semantic graph of each code snippet into a feature vector and detects Type-4 clones based on the similarity between these two vectors. To adopt the graph structure of the semantic graph, we use the graph match network (GMN) [6] to generate the feature vector of the semantic graph.

The input data of GMN are two semantic graphs (G_1, G_2) of the code pair, each semantic graph $G = (V, E)$, where V is the set of vertices and E is the set of edges. First, we initialize the feature vector of each node as $h_i^{(0)}$ using the word2vec model [11]. Moreover, we initialize data flow edges and control flow edges with different weights. Then, we calculate the node feature vectors over multiple iterations to learn the feature vectors representing the code semantics.

For each iteration t, each node updates its feature vector $h_i^{(t)}$ based on its feature vector $h_i^{(t-1)}$ in iteration $t - 1$, the message $m_i^{(t)}$ from the neighbor nodes in the same semantic graph, the similarity feature vector $\mu_i^{(t)}$ from another semantic graph. GMN uses a gated recurrent unit (GRU) [3] to update the feature vector in Eq. 1.

$$h_i^{(t)} = \mathbf{GRU}(h_i^{t-1}, m_i^{(t)}, \mu_i^{(t)}) \tag{1}$$

For node i, $m_i^{(t)}$ refers to the message from its neighbors via the edges, allowing $h_i^{(t)}$ to obtain interrelationships between the node and the entire semantic graph.

$$m_i^{(t)} = \sum_j \mathbf{SUM}(h_i^{(t)}, h_j^{(t)}, e_{ij}) \tag{2}$$

In Eq. 2, node j is a neighbor of node i in the same semantic graph, the message from node j to node i is calculated by weighted sum, and the weight is the feature vector of edge e_{ij}. Moreover, GMN adopts an attention mechanism to generate $h_i^{(t)}$ while referencing the semantic graph of another code snippet.

$$\alpha_{k \to i} = \frac{exp(s_h(h_i^{(t-1)}, h_k^{(t-1)}))}{\sum_{k'} exp(s_h(h_i^{(t-1)}, h_{k'}^{(t-1)}))} \tag{3}$$

$$\mu_i^{(t)} = \sum_k \alpha_{k \to i}(h_i^{(t-1)} - h_k^{(t-1)}) \tag{4}$$

As shown in Eq. 3, s_h is a cosine similarity metric. $h_k^{(t-1)}$ represents the feature vectors of the nodes in another semantic graph. $\alpha_{k \to i}$ refers to the similarity between node i and node k, which is used as the attention weight. $\mu_i^{(t)}$ aggregates the attention weights between the node i and all the nodes in another semantic graph and represents the attention mechanism of node i. $\mu_i^{(t)}$ allows $h_i^{(t)}$ to represent the semantics of each node with a focus based on the difference between the two semantic graphs and consequently, helps the model represent the semantics of two code snippets more precisely.

After T iterations, the feature vector of each node $h_i^{(T)}$ represents the semantics of each node and corresponding instructions. Subsequently, to represent the code semantics of the entire semantic graph, GMN aggregates the feature vector of each node into the feature vector of the semantic graph (h_G) using a multilayer perceptron (MLP) [7]. Furthermore, since the information of each node has a different contribution to the code semantics, GMN adopts the attention mechanism during the calculation of h_G.

$$\mathbf{h}_G = \mathrm{MLP}_G \left(\sum_{i \in V} \sigma \left(\mathrm{MLP}_{\mathrm{gate}} \left(\mathbf{h}_i^{(T)} \right) \right) \odot \mathrm{MLP} \left(\mathbf{h}_i^{(T)} \right) \right) \tag{5}$$

As shown in Eq. 5, $\sigma(\mathrm{MLP}_{\mathrm{gate}}(\mathbf{h}_i^{(T)}))$ represents the attention mechanism, which assigns different weights to different node feature vectors. It is trained during the training process and guides the aggregation of node feature vectors. It generates the h_G with focus, which enables it to represent code semantics more accurately.

Finally, we adopt cosine similarity to calculate the similarity between the feature vector of the two code snippets. By comparing the similarity of feature vectors and the threshold, we can predict whether the input code pair is a Type-4 clone. We choose the threshold empirically based on the validation set.

4   Experiment

In this section, we conduct experiments to evaluate our approach by answering the following research questions.

RQ1: How does SEED perform against baseline approaches?
Previous studies achieve good experimental results on their datasets [20,22]. To compare the performance of SEED with those of previous studies, we followed the experimental setup of previous studies to test the model performance.

RQ2: How does SEED perform when implemented on a more diversified dataset?
The existing datasets, although they contain numerous code pairs, the number of their semantics is relatively small. This makes code clone detectors only exposed to limited semantics, thereby posing a threat to the training and testing of the model. Accordingly, we constructed a more diversified dataset and tested the performance of SEED to understand if SEED can achieve a consistent result.

RQ3: How effective are the different semantic graph construction strategies of SEED at Type-4 clone detection?
Since SEED constructed the semantic graph while focusing on the operation. To evaluate the performance of emphasizing operator and API call tokens in semantic graph construction and make sure the semantic graph construction strategy in SEED is the best one, we carried out an ablation study on the semantic graph construction method.

4.1   Experiment Setup

Datasets. In our experiment, we use two public datasets Big-CloneBench [16] and POJ-104 [12], and one larger-scale customized dataset called CF-500. The overall information of datasets is listed in Table 1.

BigCloneBench is built by mining frequently used code semantics from *Java* project dataset, IJAdataset-2.0. We select 11,799 compilable code snippets covering 43 semantics from the BigCloneBench as one of our datasets. POJ-104 [12] is a widely used dataset to evaluate the performance of Type-4 code clone detection. It is collected from an open judging platform POJ[5], which contains many programming problems and corresponding submissions. Since submissions of the same problem in the open judging platform usually have the same semantic and different syntactic structures and therefore can be classified into Type-4 clone pairs. POJ-104 contains 104 problems and 500 submissions written in *C* for each problem. Since the submissions will be compiled and executed by the

---

[5] http://poj.org/.

open judging platform, all these submissions are compilable and thereby can be used as our dataset.

Although the existing datasets contain numerous clone pairs, they have relatively limited semantics, resulting in limited exposure to less semanticity and posing a threat to the training and testing of the model. To alleviate such a threat, we built a more diversified dataset named CF-500. We collected CF-500 from the open judging platform Codeforces[6]. CF-500 contains more than 23,000 code snippets written in C, covering 500 problems.

Since each two code snippets can construct a code pair, the number of code pairs in a dataset can be higher than 10,000,000 if using all possible combinations. Due to the vast number of code pairs, we randomly downsample the code pairs to build our datasets. For all the training sets, we sample 100,000 code pairs randomly with the proportion of the clone pairs and nonclone pairs as 1:1. For the validation set and the test set, we randomly select 10,000 code pairs from the remaining pairs.

Baseline Approaches. We reproduced two state-of-the-art approaches, ASTNN and TBCCD, to compare with our approach. ASTNN [22] proposes a novel two-step approach to represent the code snippet, using RNN to encode the AST of each statement first and transforming the AST encoding of all the statements into one vector to represent the code snippet. TBCCD [20] uses position-aware character embedding (PACE) technology to embed tokens. PACE takes the token embedding and AST as the input and generates the feature vector using tree-based LSTM to represent the code snippet. Both of them likely use the similarity of feature vectors to detect code clones. We do not compare with FA-AST [17] or Deepsim [24], since they only support *JAVA* and report similar results compared to TBCCD in their paper.

Table 1. Overall information for datasets

Datasets	Language	Semantics	Code snippets
BigCloneBench	JAVA	43	11,799
POJ-104	C	104	52,000
CF-500	C	500	23,146

4.2   Answer to RQ1: Overall Performance

In this experiment, we compare SEED's performance against two baseline approaches. Previous studies [17,18] simply split code pairs into the training, validation, and test sets to proceed with the experiment. Although such an approach ensures that code pairs in the three sets are not the same, it does not

---

[6] http://codeforces.com/.

consider the semantics of the code snippet. In other words, different implementations of the same semantics may be split into different sets, making it possible for the model to see the code snippets under the same semantics in the test set during the training process. However, the semantics vary in real-world software, and it is impossible to include all semantics in the training set. To better evaluate the performance of SEED, we split the training, validation, and test sets from different code semantics.

Following the setting in TBCCD [20], we use two public datasets, Big-CloneBench and POJ-104, to evaluate the model performance. We construct the training set and the validation set from their first 15 problems and 10 problems. Instead of using all the remaining problems as the test set, we divided them into 6 and 3 test sets to evaluate the robustness of SEED when testing different semantics. We illustrate the experimental results in Table 2. Columns P, R, and $F1$ represent precision, recall, and F1-Score, respectively.

We find that SEED significantly outperforms both baseline approaches on all test sets. On POJ-104, SEED obtains an average F1-Score of 0.62, which is higher than the F1-Score of ASTNN (0.45) and TBCCD (0.50). Compared with TBCCD, SEED outperforms by at least 17.5% (from 0.40 to 0.47) in the form of the F1-Score in the test set with problem IDs 16–30 and even by approximately 30% (from 0.53 to 0.68) in the form of F1-Score in the test set with problem IDs 61–75. For BigCloneBench, similarly, SEED achieves an average F1-Score of 0.54, which significantly outperforms that of baseline approaches. In particular, in terms of precision, SEED outperforms baselines by 74.4% on average. In the real-world software repositories, the accuracy of clone pairs reported by SEED is higher than the accuracy of baselines. Compared with the performance on POJ-104, the F1-Scores of baselines in BigCloneBench drop by approximately 25%, while those of SEED drop by less than 15% because BigCloneBench is collected from a practical software environment in which the identifiers and API calls vary. Although exciting improvement of SEED in precision, recall, and F1-score, we must acknowledge that SEED performs poorer robustness than baselines, since the F1-score of SEED drops 34% (from 0.71 to 0.47), while that of TBCCD and ASTNN only drops 28% (from 0.56 to 0.40) and 29% (from 0.51 to 0.36) in different test sets.

4.3   Answer to RQ2: Larger-scale Experiment

In this experiment, we aimed to alleviate the threat caused by the small number of the semantics of the existing dataset and evaluate the performance of our approach over the more diversified datasets, CF-500. Since the experiment setting in previous studies [18,20] and RQ1 only use a limited size of datasets, we also use the entire POJ-104 and BigCloneBench dataset to do an experiment and analyze the result.

To understand the robustness of SEED in different sizes of dataset, We keep the validation set and test set unchanged and train the model on varied training sets. For BigCloneBench, we extract a validation set from semantic IDs 32–37 and a test set from semantic IDs 38–44. The training sets are built from

Table 2. Result of SEED and other baselines on the POJ-104 and BigCloneBench dataset

Datasets	Problem IDs for testing	ASTNN			TBCCD			SEED		
		P	R	F1	P	R	F1	P	R	F1
POJ-104	16–30	0.32	0.42	0.36	0.35	0.46	0.40	**0.41**	**0.57**	**0.47**
	31–45	0.44	0.61	0.51	0.51	0.62	0.56	**0.74**	**0.68**	**0.71**
	45–60	0.41	**0.60**	0.49	0.59	0.48	0.53	**0.71**	0.60	**0.64**
	61–75	0.41	0.65	0.51	0.58	0.49	0.53	**0.78**	**0.69**	**0.68**
	76–90	0.38	**0.63**	0.47	0.61	0.44	0.51	**0.71**	0.57	**0.63**
	(91–104) + 16	0.37	0.45	0.40	0.48	0.45	0.46	**0.61**	**0.55**	**0.58**
	Average	0.39	0.56	0.45	0.52	0.49	0.50	**0.66**	**0.61**	**0.64**
BigCloneBench	12–22	0.28	0.39	0.32	0.20	**0.92**	0.33	**0.58**	0.44	**0.50**
	23–33	0.34	0.40	0.37	0.27	**0.91**	0.41	**0.72**	0.57	**0.63**
	34–44	0.25	0.30	0.27	0.17	**0.67**	0.27	**0.44**	0.51	**0.47**
	Average	0.29	0.36	0.33	0.21	**0.83**	0.38	**0.58**	0.51	**0.54**

semantics IDs 2–11, 2–21, and 2–31. For POJ-104, we set problem IDs 76–90 as the validation set and problem IDs 91–104 as the test set. Then, we create several training sets of different sizes. The training sets cover problem IDs 1–15, 1–30, 1–45, 1–60, and 1–75. For CF-500, we set problem IDs 401–450 and 451–500 as the validation set and test set, and problem IDs 1–100, 1–200, 1–300, and 1–400 as training sets, providing us with a series of training sets of increasing size from 10 to 400.

Table 3. Result of SEED and other baselines on the more diversified datasets

Datasets	Problem IDs for training	ASTNN			TBCCD			SEED		
		P	R	F1	P	R	F1	P	R	F1
POJ-104	1–15	0.36	0.48	0.41	0.40	0.63	0.49	**0.51**	**0.64**	**0.57**
	1–30	0.44	0.52	0.50	0.51	**0.71**	0.59	**0.74**	0.66	**0.70**
	1–45	0.49	0.69	0.57	0.61	**0.71**	0.65	**0.80**	0.67	**0.73**
	1–60	0.55	**0.80**	0.65	0.69	0.66	0.67	**0.78**	0.74	**0.76**
	1–75	0.61	**0.83**	0.66	0.70	0.69	0.70	**0.77**	0.78	**0.78**
BigCloneBench	2–11	0.30	0.33	0.31	0.21	**0.71**	0.32	**0.50**	0.55	**0.52**
	2–21	0.34	0.47	0.39	0.30	**0.69**	0.42	**0.57**	0.68	**0.62**
	2–31	0.36	0.55	0.43	0.33	**0.69**	0.45	**0.68**	0.68	**0.68**
CF-500	1–100	0.63	**0.85**	0.72	0.71	0.77	0.74	**0.82**	0.74	**0.78**
	1–200	0.62	**0.87**	0.73	0.73	0.76	0.74	**0.80**	0.80	**0.80**
	1–300	0.62	**0.89**	0.74	0.73	0.77	0.75	**0.81**	0.82	**0.81**
	1–400	0.61	**0.94**	0.74	0.74	0.76	0.75	**0.81**	0.83	**0.82**

As illustrated in Table 3, we find that SEED outperforms baseline approaches in all datasets. In BigCloneBench and POJ-104, SEED achieves a significant performance improvement by 54% and 14% on average in terms of the F1-Score, respectively. In particular, despite the greater number of semantics in CF-500, SEED still outperforms other approaches by 8% in the form of the F1-Score. Similar to the result of RQ1, SEED achieves the highest precision in baseline approaches while maintaining a similar recall, validating the result we discussed in RQ1 and proving that our approach can achieve a constant result when tested on more diversified datasets.

Furthermore, the results also prove that our extended dataset can alleviate the threat posed by the low number of the semantics of datasets. In BigCloneBench, with the increasing size of the dataset, the performance of SEED increases by up to 31%, 24%, and 36% in the form of F1-Score, Recall, and Precision, respectively. Likely, on POJ-104, with the increasing size of the dataset, the metrics of SEED increase by up to 37%, 21%, and 51%, respectively. In contrast, with the increasing size of the dataset in CF-500, the precision of SEED remains stable, while the F1-Score and recall increase 5% and 24%, respectively. To understand such improvement, we analyze code pairs that are correctly determined only after the dataset is expanded. The code snippets in BigCloneBench are collected from the real-world project and implement the semantics using mainly the API calls. The clone detection model can better understand the semantics of API calls by training on a more semantic-diverse dataset. For POJ-104 and CF-500, code snippets focus on the algorithm. Training on a more semantically diverse dataset enables the model to better identify the core structures of the code snippets and ignore irrelevant ones. Therefore, the result indicates that training code clone models with a semantics diverse dataset can help improve the model performance.

To establish a better understanding of the effect of dataset size on the performance of the model, we compared the performance of SEED with baseline approaches using datasets of different sizes. We found that the performance of all models increases as the size of the training set grows. Meanwhile, as the size of the dataset increases, the speed of performance improvement gradually decreases and peaks when the dataset reaches a certain size, indicating that the performance improvement caused by the size of the dataset is limited when it reaches a certain number. Moreover, we find that SEED outperforms baseline approaches over various sizes of datasets and can achieve the same performance as baselines by training on a smaller dataset, also verifying the validity of our approach.

4.4   Answer to RQ3: Ablation Study

An ablation study usually refers to comparing the performance of different strategies. Since we focus on the operator and API call tokens when constructing the semantic graph, to verify the validity of this method, we carried out an ablation study to evaluate the semantic graph construction method. We use the same dataset as RQ2. For the experimental group, we constructed different semantic graphs by combining the identifiers and data types in the semantic graphs. The setting of these semantic graphs is as follows:

- SEED+identifier: SEED+identifier uses not only the operator and API call tokens, but also identifier tokens of variables as the nodes in the semantic graph and connects data flow edges from each identifier node to its corresponding operation node.
- SEED+type: SEED+type still introduces variables as nodes in the semantic graph, while it replaces the identifier tokens of variables by the data type tokens of them.
- SEED: SEED removes all the variable or data type token, and only uses the operator and API call tokens as the node in the semantic graph.

The results of our experiments are shown in Table 4. To explore the reason for different performances when using different semantic graph construction methods, we collected the changed sizes of the constructed semantic graph and compared the differences among them. The changed sizes of different semantic graphs are shown in Table 5. The column *ratio* refers to the maximum decrease ratio between SEED and the other two models.

First, we compared the performance of SEED+identifier and SEED+type to discuss the influence of using tokens without instructive semantics in Type-4 Clone.

Table 4. Result of SEED and other settings of semantic graph on the different datasets

Datasets	Problem IDs for training	SEED+identifier			SEED+type			SEED		
		P	R	F1	P	R	F1	P	R	F1
POJ-104	1–75	0.77	0.71	0.74	**0.78**	0.75	0.76	0.77	**0.78**	**0.78**
BigCloneBench	2–31	0.50	0.57	0.53	0.64	0.61	0.62	**0.68**	**0.68**	**0.68**
CF-500	1–400	0.74	**0.83**	0.79	0.77	0.82	0.80	**0.81**	**0.83**	**0.82**

The results show that using identifiers leads to a slight performance drop of approximately 2.6% over POJ-104 and CF-500. However, using identifiers reduces the model performance in the form of F1-Score by approximately 17% in BigCloneBench. To understand such differences, we studied the semantic graph size of the three models. From Table 5, we found that after replacing identifiers by their data types (SEED+identifier and SEED+type), the size of vocabulary decreased 58,941. This result indicates that although the code snippet in BigCloneBench has good naming rules such as the *Camel case* , it still introduces noise into the dataset and leads to the out-of-vocabulary problem. In contrast, code snippets in POJ-104 and CF-500 are written by only one programmer for one simple task, making the programmer often use simple characters such as i, j, etc., resulting in a small size of the vocabulary and alleviating the out-of-vocabulary problem and preventing the model from a significant performance drop.

Second, the performance between SEED+type and SEED illustrates the effectiveness of the size of the semantic graph. For POJ-104 and CF-500, the

F1-Score increases by approximately 2%, while for BigCloneBench, the F1-Score increases by 10%. We studied the reason for this difference. Table 5 shows the content of the semantic graph in SEED+type and the content of the semantic graph in SEED. We found that by constructing a semantic graph without identifiers except for constants, the number of operand nodes and data flow edges in the semantic graph decrease by over 60% in all three datasets because SEED uses the only operation to construct the semantic graph, which significantly reduces the size of the semantic graph. With a smaller size semantic graph, the GMN model can focus on learning the semantic information (i.e., operation) in the semantic graph, resulting in a more accurate feature vector generated by GMN and consequently the improvement of the model performance.

In conclusion, the results in RQ3 indicate that the semantic graph construction strategy in SEED outperforms alternative strategies in terms of most metrics over all three datasets, proving that the semantic graph focusing on the operations can better represent the code semantics.

Table 5. The changed size of SEED's semantic graph and other settings of semantic graph on the different datasets

Datasets	Characteristic	SEED+identifier	SEED+type	SEED	Ratio
POJ-104	Vocabulary size	6204	2350	1981	0.68
	Operand node	126.83	126.83	43.84	0.65
	Dataflow edge	426.48	426.48	153.10	0.64
BigClone-Bench	vocabulary size	87,534	28,593	13,666	0.83
	Operand node	97.44	97.44	38.13	0.61
	Dataflow edge	145.93	145.93	51.58	0.64
CF-500	vocabulary size	7392	3175	2022	0.72
	Operand node	74.51	74.51	24.77	0.67
	Dataflow edge	294.74	294.74	97.98	0.67

5   Threats to Validity

In this section, we discuss the threat to the validity of our approach. SEED may suffer from two threats to validity as follows:

Internal Validity. During semantic graph construction, we emphasize operator and API call tokens of IR instruction, based on the assumption that the semantic of operator and API call tokens perform more robust compared to identifier tokens. Different API calls may have similar functionality or in reverse, which affects the performance of SEED. To verify the validity of the assumption and the strategy in semantic graph construction, we do an ablation study in Sect. 4.

External Validity. We built a Type-4 code clone dataset CF-500 in our experiment. To make sure different problems refer to different functionalities, we compare the description of each problem and discard problems with the same descriptions. However, we can not guarantee whether different problem descriptions mean different functionalities.

6 Conclusion

In this study, we presented a semantic-based deep detection approach, SEED, to detect Type-4 code clones. SEED focused on the semantic structure of code and the operator and API call tokens. To alleviate the threat posed by the small number of functionalities in the previous dataset, we constructed a dataset, CF-500, containing 23,146 code implementations of 500 functionalities. This dataset is nearly five times the size of the existing dataset. Extensive experiments over two public datasets and one customized dataset show that our approach, compared to the 3 baseline approaches, achieves state-of-the-art performance. Our approach can be applied in practice to assist with software maintenance.

In the future, we aim to further improve the performance of the tool supporting your approach. To better represent the semantics of the source code, we can filter out more less-semantic content from the semantic graph, and merge more semantic features in it. Another potential extension to our work is to leverage other GNN models, which can better compare the semantic graphs and embed them into feature vectors.

Acknowledgements. The authors would like to thank the anonymous reviewers for their insightful comments. This work was substantially supported by National Natural Science Foundation of China (No. 61872373 and 61872375).

References

1. Antoniol, G., Villano, U., Merlo, E., Di Penta, M.: Analyzing cloning evolution in the Linux kernel. Inf. Softw. Technol. **44**(13), 755–765 (2002)
2. Ben-Nun, T., Jakobovits, A.S., Hoefler, T.: Neural code comprehension: a learnable representation of code semantics. Adv. Neural Inf. Process. Syst. **31**, 3585–3597 (2018)
3. Cho, K., et al.: Learning phrase representations using rnn encoder-decoder for statistical machine translation. arXiv preprint arXiv:1406.1078 (2014)
4. Jiang, L., Misherghi, G., Su, Z., Glondu, S.: Deckard: scalable and accurate tree-based detection of code clones. In: 29th International Conference on Software Engineering (ICSE 2007), pp. 96–105. IEEE (2007)
5. Li, X., Wang, L., Xin, Y., Yang, Y., Chen, Y.: Automated vulnerability detection in source code using minimum intermediate representation learning. Appl. Sci. **10**(5), 1692 (2020)
6. Li, Y., Gu, C., Dullien, T., Vinyals, O., Kohli, P.: Graph matching networks for learning the similarity of graph structured objects. In: International Conference on Machine Learning, pp. 3835–3845. PMLR (2019)

7. Li, Y., Tarlow, D., Brockschmidt, M., Zemel, R.: Gated graph sequence neural networks. arXiv preprint arXiv:1511.05493 (2015)
8. Li, Z., Lu, S., Myagmar, S., Zhou, Y.: Cp-miner: finding copy-paste and related bugs in large-scale software code. IEEE Trans. Softw. Eng. **32**(3), 176–192 (2006)
9. Linstead, E., Bajracharya, S., Ngo, T., Rigor, P., Lopes, C., Baldi, P.: Sourcerer: mining and searching internet-scale software repositories. Data Min. Knowl. Disc. **18**(2), 300–336 (2009)
10. Mazinanian, D., Tsantalis, N., Stein, R., Valenta, Z.: Jdeodorant: clone refactoring. In: Proceedings of the 38th International Conference on Software Engineering Companion, pp. 613–616 (2016)
11. Mikolov, T., Chen, K., Corrado, G., Dean, J.: Efficient estimation of word representations in vector space. arXiv preprint arXiv:1301.3781 (2013)
12. Mou, L., Li, G., Zhang, L., Wang, T., Jin, Z.: Convolutional neural networks over tree structures for programming language processing. In: Proceedings of the AAAI Conference on Artificial Intelligence, vol. 30 (2016)
13. Pizzolotto, D., Inoue, K.: Blanker: a refactor-oriented cloned source code normalizer. In: 2020 IEEE 14th International Workshop on Software Clones (IWSC), pp. 22–25. IEEE (2020)
14. Roy, C.K., Cordy, J.R., Koschke, R.: Comparison and evaluation of code clone detection techniques and tools: a qualitative approach. Sci. Comput. Program. **74**(7), 470–495 (2009)
15. Saini, V., Farmahinifarahani, F., Lu, Y., Baldi, P., Lopes, C.V.: Oreo: detection of clones in the twilight zone. In: Proceedings of the 2018 26th ACM Joint Meeting on European Software Engineering Conference and Symposium on the Foundations of Software Engineering, pp. 354–365 (2018)
16. Svajlenko, J., Islam, J.F., Keivanloo, I., Roy, C.K., Mia, M.M.: Towards a big data curated benchmark of inter-project code clones. In: 2014 IEEE International Conference on Software Maintenance and Evolution, pp. 476–480. IEEE (2014)
17. Wang, W., Li, G., Ma, B., Xia, X., Jin, Z.: Detecting code clones with graph neural network and flow-augmented abstract syntax tree. In: 2020 IEEE 27th International Conference on Software Analysis, Evolution and Reengineering (SANER), pp. 261–271. IEEE (2020)
18. Wei, H., Li, M.: Supervised deep features for software functional clone detection by exploiting lexical and syntactical information in source code. In: IJCAI, pp. 3034–3040 (2017)
19. White, M., Tufano, M., Vendome, C., Poshyvanyk, D.: Deep learning code fragments for code clone detection. In: 2016 31st IEEE/ACM International Conference on Automated Software Engineering (ASE), pp. 87–98. IEEE (2016)
20. Yu, H., Lam, W., Chen, L., Li, G., Xie, T., Wang, Q.: Neural detection of semantic code clones via tree-based convolution. In: 2019 IEEE/ACM 27th International Conference on Program Comprehension (ICPC), pp. 70–80. IEEE (2019)
21. Zeng, C., et al.: degraphcs: embedding variable-based flow graph for neural code search. arXiv preprint arXiv:2103.13020 (2021)
22. Zhang, J., Wang, X., Zhang, H., Sun, H., Wang, K., Liu, X.: A novel neural source code representation based on abstract syntax tree. In: 2019 IEEE/ACM 41st International Conference on Software Engineering (ICSE), pp. 783–794. IEEE (2019)
23. Zhang, L., Yan, L., Zhang, Z., Zhang, J., Chan, W., Zheng, Z.: A theoretical analysis on cloning the failed test cases to improve spectrum-based fault localization. J. Syst. Softw. **129**, 35–57 (2017)

24. Zhao, G., Huang, J.: Deepsim: deep learning code functional similarity. In: Proceedings of the 2018 26th ACM Joint Meeting on European Software Engineering Conference and Symposium on the Foundations of Software Engineering, pp. 141–151 (2018)
25. Zou, Y., Ban, B., Xue, Y., Xu, Y.: CCGraph: a PDG-based code clone detector with approximate graph matching. In: 2020 35th IEEE/ACM International Conference on Automated Software Engineering (ASE), pp. 931–942. IEEE (2020)

Barriers to Device Longevity and Reuse: An Analysis of Application Download, Installation and Functionality on a Vintage Device

Craig Goodwin(✉) and Sandra Woolley

Keele University, Keele, Staffordshire, UK
c.goodwin@keele.ac.uk

Abstract. This paper contributes a methodology and analysis of application installation and function on a 'vintage' device. Attempts were made to download, install, open, and run 230 apps on an Apple iPad Mini tablet of approximately nine years old. The apps comprised the top 10 of each of 23 major app categories from the Apple App Store. Of the total of 230 apps, only 29 could be downloaded directly to the device and, of these, 24 were functional. Significantly, a further 140 apps *could* be downloaded indirectly via a newer (non-vintage) Apple device. Of these indirectly downloaded apps, 135 installed and opened on the vintage device, and 117 were functional. In summary, despite only 29 (12.6%) of top 10 apps being directly downloadable for vintage devices via the Apple App Store, a total of 141 (61.3%) were capable of functioning. These results highlight some of the difficulties experienced by vintage device users and the barriers to device longevity and, to some extent, the unnecessary and premature nature of device obsolescence. We discuss measures Apple and developers could take to prolong support for legacy devices that could prevent functional devices from becoming e-waste and prolong their use and/or reuse.

Keywords: Device reuse · Software reuse · E-waste · Digital sustainability · Legacy applications

1 Introduction

Approximately 53 million metric tons of electronic waste are currently produced every year, and this is expected to rise to 75 million tons by 2030 [1]. Despite many electronic devices being recyclable, only 15–20% are typically recycled and most are disposed of in landfill after being discarded because of obstacles to their continued use. For example, there are barriers to repair such as device warranty limitations and the technically demanding nature of repairs that are beyond many consumers, with the result that devices are no longer functional in today's IoT and are discarded for convenience [1, 2].

© Springer Nature Switzerland AG 2022
G. Perrouin et al. (Eds.): ICSR 2022, LNCS 13297, pp. 138–145, 2022.
https://doi.org/10.1007/978-3-031-08129-3_9

Apple Inc. is the market leader in the technology sector with an estimated market capitalization of 3 trillion US dollars [3]. New models of Apple iPhone smartphones have been released every year since 2007 [4] and Apple's tablet devices have been updated on an annual basis since 2010 [4]. Schemes such as the iPhone Upgrade Plan [5] enable consumers to receive new iPhones yearly and return their 'old' device [6]. Apple publish annual Environmental Progress Reports and have announced a commitment to a 2030 carbon neutral goal [6, 7]. But little is known in general about the second life of devices that are refurbished, recycled, or disposed in landfill or as e-waste (dependent on device condition).

The motivation for the study presented here was to explore device obsolescence and glean insights into the extent of challenges of continued device use. Significant barriers to continued use of older devices are i) a lack of compatibility with new and updated apps and ii) a lack of information about compatibility. App store application details regarding compatibility, whilst generally useful, aren't always a reliable source of information for vintage devices users Importantly, at the time of writing, the only method of discovering whether an app downloads and functions on a vintage iOS device is to manually attempt downloading each app. The study presented in this paper exemplifies the challenge of continued device use with a 'vintage' Apple Mini tablet.

2   Background

There is a lack of research and innovation in legacy device use and reuse. Additionally, there is little academic literature on end-of-life devices. In contrast there is a significant amount of grey literature discussing device reuse which helps contextualize the research area. For example, there are consumer guides for repurposing and reusing older smart devices [8–12], but these do not address meaningful reuse strategies (i.e., actual device use/reuse or ethical recycling). In terms of device ownership behaviors, iPhone users are more likely to sell or trade their old device than Android users [13], but approximately 30% of iPhone users keep their old devices [13]. Statistics such as these highlight the importance of researching the longevity and use/reuse of older devices [14] (and furthermore topics such as functionality, accessibility, and e-waste) in the wider context of the circular economy [15].

Since 2010, much has been discussed regarding device reuse and reuse models [16]. Of course, this can be due to the reason that smart devices are only now starting to become "obsolete" in use [17, 18]. Boano [19] proposes increasing the durability and support of legacy devices to "avoid an 'Internet of Trash' concluding that it is *"important to study how to increase the lifetime of IoT devices that have become obsolete or no longer compatible with the latest communication standards, so to prevent an early disposal."* Safe disposal of these devices is also a contentious issue, as often sensitive data can be retrieved from devices that have been sold by consumers [21], sent for refurbishment [22] or recycled [20, 23, 24].

Despite recent interest in app store business models, for example, as evidenced by the proposed US Congress Open Act Markets antitrust bill and the Fortnite vs. Google lawsuit [25], there is a persistent lack of research and interest for increasing device lifespans and extending device support by manufacturers and developers. This furthers the need for research exploration in the practice and drivers of 'sideloading', which is defined as the download and installation of apps outside of official smartphone app marketplaces [26].

3   Methods

This study aimed to investigate the barriers to device and software usage and the obstacles to app installation that users of vintage devices may experience. The vintage device used in the study was an Apple iPad Mini tablet (iOS version 9.3.6) of approximately nine years old at the time of the study which took place September 30th to October 2nd, 2021.

For indirect downloading, an Apple iPhone SE (iOS version 15.1, 'currently supported' at the time of the study) was used. This device allows us to download the required app (sharing the same account with the vintage iPad Mini) and then use the iPad Mini to view the account purchase history to download the last supported version of that app (if supported and applicable). From there, we checked whether the app successfully downloaded, installed, and functioned on the iPad Mini. This methodology is summarized in Fig. 1.

The 2012 iPad Mini vintage device used for the study is significant due to it being the last 32-bit Apple Tablet [4]. This era (2012) positions the device as "vintage" but not "obsolete" according to Apple's definition: *"Products are considered vintage when Apple stopped distributing them for sale more than 5 and less than 7 years ago"* [27].

3.1   App Selection Criteria and Collection

Major app categories (23 in total) from the Apple App Store were selected. The app category "Kids" was excluded because the category consolidates other app types into one category. In addition, categories which are now included on modern Apple devices ("Apple Watch Apps", "AR Apps", "Developer Tools", "Graphics & Design" and "Safari Extensions") were excluded because they do not feature on the Apple Mini Tablet App store. Additional criteria for App selection is listed in the Appendix.

4   Results

As shown in Fig. 1 the results of the study show a large and distinct difference be-tween apps that can be downloaded directly vs apps that can be downloaded via the help of another device vs apps that couldn't be downloaded either way (~12.6% vs ~68.9% vs ~26.5%). There was also a high uptake of previous app support, as 31 apps were never compatible with the study device. As shown in Fig. 2, the categories with the highest number of apps that could be directly downloaded were "Magazines" and "Books" (5 and 4) which is to be expected as these are less device intensive apps and therefore can usually be supported by developers for a longer period.

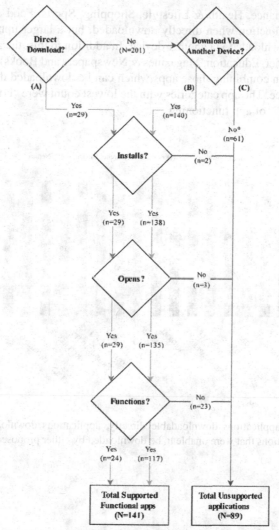

Fig. 1. App function flowchart outlining the study method and results: (A): Apps downloaded directly (*green*). (B): Apps downloaded via another device (*yellow*). (C): Apps that could not be downloaded directly via another device (or no previous support for the test device (*red*) and that failed "Installs?", "Opens?" and "Functions?" (*34 of the apps were never supported by the device iOS version.*) (Color figure online)

4.1 Functional Supported Apps and Unsupported Apps

In total, 141 functional supported apps could be installed in comparison to the 89 unsupported apps (61.3% vs 38.7%). These figures indicate a much lower percentage compared to apps that could be downloaded but are still indicative of a device that has a good level of app support even if it is defined as "vintage". Comparing the functionality of app categories (see Fig. 3), the app categories comprising: Music, News, Business, Photo &

Video, Travel, Finance, Health & Lifestyle, Shopping, Sports, Food & Drink, had no apps that would function when directly downloaded, but a larger uptake in app functionality when downloaded via another device. In addition to this, the app categories of (Reference, Weather, Education, Magazines & Newspapers and Books) had at least 80% functionality when combining those apps which can be downloaded directly and those with another device. The app categories with the lowest count were "Food & Drink" and "Games" with 10% of app functioning.

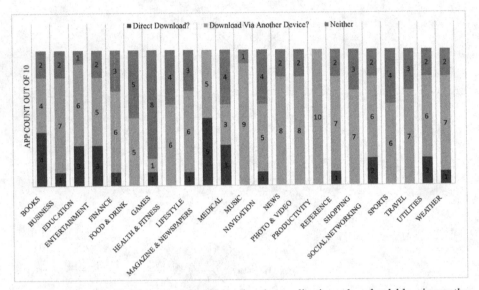

Fig. 2. Count of applications downloadable directly, applications downloadable via another device and applications that were unable to be downloaded by either proposed method.

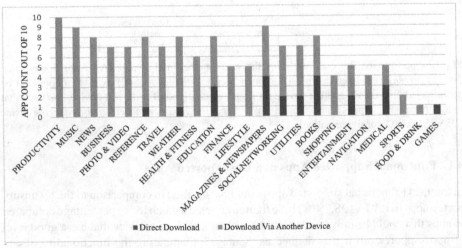

Fig. 3. Supported functional apps sorted by categories & stacked by download method.

5 Conclusion

The study identifies significant issues in device and software reuse. By testing the down-loading and functionality of 230 apps across 23 app categories, this study has demon-strated a considerable difference between the number of apps that could be downloaded directly (29) vs the number of applications that could be downloaded indirectly via another device (140). This research highlights barriers of app usage in context to vintage Apple devices and helps provide evidence that little is being done to promote and extend the support and compatibility lifespan of these devices. The hurdles involved in testing app compatibility on vintage devices is not consumer friendly and requires manual input and discovery.

Whilst the majority of iPhone and iPad users will upgrade to newer hardware iter-ations of Apple products, there is still a sizable contingency who remain users of older devices (using iOS 12 or earlier). It is recommended that application developers and Apple Inc. increase the transparency of app compatibility for vintage device users. It is advised that access to incompatible or non-supported apps on these devices is closed.

Nevertheless, the focus of this study was not to assess the functionality of apps in certain categories (as this figure will decrease over time for the study device), but rather to highlight the issues that legacy device users face in prolonging the use and reuse of their older devices. Research and testing of vintage and obsolete devices using this methodology is recommended to further explore the use and reuse of devices and software to underpin continued device use/reuse.

Appendix

Additional App Selection Criteria

- Apps were required to have cross-platform support, i.e., apps exclusive to a subset of Apple devices were not selected.
- The app appears as 'available to download' on the iPad Mini App Store.
- The app is in the Top 10-Free apps of its respective category (e.g., Travel.) as of September 30th to October 2nd (these were identified on September 30th as Apple change the Top 10 list regularly).
- No attention will be made specific application device or iOS requirements. Current or Previous App support will be defined and considered after the study is completed.
- The app categories "Magazines & Newspapers" and "News" often contain the same apps, therefore the top 10 of "Magazines & Newspapers" will be selected first and then the top 10 of "News" will be selected. Should a duplicate exist then the next available app will be selected.

References

1. Forti, V., Balde, C.P., Kuehr, R., Bel, G.: The global E-waste monitor 2020: quantities, flows and the circular economy potential (2020)
2. Royal Society of Chemistry. Elements in danger. Royal Society of Chemistry (online) (2019). https://www.rsc.org/new-perspectives/sustainability/elements-in-danger/#surveyfindings
3. Smith, Z.S.: Apple Becomes 1st Company Worth $3 Trillion—Greater Than The GDP Of The UK. (online) Forbes (2022). https://www.forbes.com/sites/zacharysmith/2022/01/03/apple-becomes-1st-company-worth-3-trillion-greater-than-the-gdp-of-the-uk/?sh=83f4975603fc. Accessed 19 Jan 2022
4. Apple Discussions. Complete List of iPads, release year and current iOS / iPad Os version they can run. - Apple Community. (online) discussions.apple.com (2022). https://discussions.apple.com/docs/DOC-250001726
5. Apple. iPhone Upgrade Program. (online) Apple (2022). https://www.apple.com/shop/iphone/iphone-upgrade-program
6. Apple (UK). Apple Trade In. (online) (2022). https://www.apple.com/uk/shop/trade-in?afid=p238%7CsrZLBWyVZ-dc_mtid_187079nc38483_pcrid_436885031988_pgrid_101811355112_&cid=aos-uk-kwgo-Tradein--slid---product. Accessed 18 Jan 2022
7. Apple. Environmental Progress Report. (online) (2021). https://www.apple.com/euro/environment/pdf/a/generic/Apple_Environmental_Progress_Report_2021.pdf
8. Crossl, Y., Rawlinson, N.: What to do with your old tech. (online) Good Housekeeping (2021). https://www.goodhousekeeping.com/uk/consumer-advice/technology/a26422571/what-to-do-with-old-tech-gadgets/. Accessed 4 Jan 2022
9. Raphael, J.R.: 20 great uses for an old Android device. (online) Computerworld (2019). https://www.computerworld.com/article/2487680/20-great-uses-for-an-old-android-device.html. Accessed 4 Jan 2022
10. Contributor, R.Y.: 10 Ways to Reuse an Old iPad. (online) Rocket Yard (2020). https://eshop.macsales.com/blog/63303-10-ways-to-reuse-an-old-ipad/. Accessed 4 Jan 2022
11. Broida, R.: 6 new uses for your old iPad. (online) CNET (2019). https://www.cnet.com/tech/computing/6-new-uses-for-your-old-ipad/. Accessed 4 Jan 2022
12. Peterson, M.: 7 creative ways to repurpose and reuse your old iPhones and iPads. (online) AppleToolBox (2020). https://appletoolbox.com/7-creative-ways-to-repurpose-and-reuse-your-old-iphones-and-ipads/. Accessed 4 Jan 2022
13. Espósito, F.: Report: iPhone owners more likely to sell or trade in their old devices than Android users. (online) 9to5Mac (2021). https://9to5mac.com/2021/09/13/report-iphone-owners-more-likely-to-sell-or-trade-in-their-old-devices-than-android-users/. Accessed 1 Feb 2022
14. Bischoff, P.: 1 in 5 secondhand mobile phones still contain data from previous owners: report. (online) Comparitech (2019). https://www.comparitech.com/blog/information-security/personal-data-left-on-mobile-phones/. Accessed 1 Feb 2022
15. Kirchherr, J., Reike, D., Hekkert, M.: Conceptualizing the circular economy: an analysis of 114 definitions. Resour. Conserv. Recycl. **127**, 221–232 (2017)
16. Li, X., et al.: Smartphone evolution and reuse: establishing a more sustainable model. In: 2010 39th International Conference on Parallel Processing Workshops, pp. 476–484 (2010). https://doi.org/10.1109/ICPPW.2010.70
17. Hazelwood, D.A., Pecht, M.G.: Life extension of electronic products: a case study of smartphones. IEEE Access **9**, 144726–144739 (2021). https://doi.org/10.1109/ACCESS.2021.3121733
18. Venables, R.: The Smartphone Replacement Cycle. (online) Phoenix Cellular (2021). https://phoenixcellular.com/news/the-smartphone-replacement-cycle/

19. Boano, C.: Enabling support of legacy devices for a more sustainable internet of things: a position paper on the need to proactively avoid an "Internet of Trash". In: Proceedings of the Conference on Information Technology for Social Good (GoodIT 2021), Association for Computing Machinery, New York, pp. 97–102 (2021). https://doi.org/10.1145/3462203.3475883

20. Makov, T., Fitzpatrick, C.: Is repairability enough? Big data insights into smartphone obsolescence and consumer interest in repair. J. Clean. Prod. **313**, 127561 (2021)

21. Makov, T., Fishman, T., Chertow, M.R., Blass, V.: What affects the secondhand value of smartphones: evidence from eBay. J. Ind. Ecol. **23**(3), 549–559 (2018)

22. Debnath, B., Das, A., Das, S., Das, A.: Studies on security threats in waste mobile phone recycling supply chain in India. IEEE Calcutta Conf. (CALCON) **2020**, 431–434 (2020). https://doi.org/10.1109/CALCON49167.2020.9106531

23. Cook, D.M., Dissanayake, D.N., Kaur, K.: The usability factors of lost digital legacy data from regulatory misconduct: older values and the issue of ownership. In: 2019 7th International Conference on Information and Communication Technology (ICoICT), pp. 1–6 (2019). https://doi.org/10.1109/ICoICT.2019.8835309

24. Newman, B., Al-Nemrat, A.: Making the internet of things sustainable: an evidence based practical approach in finding solutions for yet to be discussed challenges in the internet of things. In: Montasari, R., Jahankhani, H., Hill, R., Parkinson, S. (eds.) Digital Forensic Investigation of Internet of Things (IoT) Devices. ASTSA, pp. 255–285. Springer, Cham (2021). https://doi.org/10.1007/978-3-030-60425-7_11

25. Blumenthal, R.: Open App Markets Act, S.2710 - 117th Congress (2021–2022): Open App Markets Act. (online) (2021). www.congress.gov, https://www.congress.gov/bill/117th-congress/senate-bill/2710?s=1&r=23

26. Goodwin, C.: "Why sideload?" User behaviours, interactions and accessibility issues around mobile app installation. In: Proceedings of the 33rd International BCS Human Computer Interaction Conference, (online) (2020). https://www.scienceopen.com/hosted-document?, https://doi.org/10.14236/ewic/HCI20DC.5. Accessed 8 Jan 2022

27. Apple. Vintage and obsolete products. (online) Apple Support (2021). https://support.apple.com/en-gb/HT201624

Author Index

Printed in the United States
by Baker & Taylor Publisher Services